1992

Springer Series on ADULTHOOD and AGING

Series Editor: Bernard D. Starr, Ph.D.

Advisory Board: Paul D. Baltes, Ph.D., Jack Botwinick, Ph.D., Carl Eisdorfer, Ph.D., M.D., Donald E. Gelfand, Ph.D., Lissy Jarvik, M.D., Ph.D., Robert Kastenbaum, Ph.D., Neil G. McCluskey, Ph.D., K. Warner Schaie, Ph.D., Nathan W. Shock, Ph.D., and Asher Woldow, M.D.

Erdman B. Palmore, PhD, was born in Japan of missionary parents and was raised in Virginia. He received a BA from Duke University, an MA from the University of Chicago, and a PhD from Columbia University, all in sociology.

He taught at Finch College and Yale University and did research for the Social Security Administration prior to joining the faculty at Duke University in 1967. At Duke he has been coordinator for the Duke Longitudinal Studies and principal investigator of several research projects. He is now Professor of Medical Sociology and a Senior Fellow at the Duke Center for the Study of Aging and Human Development.

Dr. Palmore has written or edited 14 books, including the *Normal Aging* series, *International Handbook on the Aged, Handbook on the Aged in the U.S., The Honorable Elders Revisited, Retirement: Causes and Consequences,* and *The Facts on Aging Quiz: A Handbook of Uses and Results,* the last two published by Springer Publishing Company. He has also written 16 chapters in other books and over 80 articles in professional journals. His books and papers have received several awards. He is a Fellow of both the American Sociological Society and the Gerontological Society of America and has served as president of the Southern Gerontological Society. He received an award for Distinguished Gerontologists for 1989 by the Southern Gerontological Society. His research and teaching interests include race relations, retirement, longevity, life satisfaction, health, and international gerontology.

AGEISM
Negative and Positive

Erdman B. Palmore

SPRINGER PUBLISHING COMPANY
New York

Springer Publishing Company, Inc.
536 Broadway
New York, NY 10012

90 91 92 93 94 / 5 4 3 2 1

Library of Congress Cataloging-in-Publication Data
Palmore, Erdman Ballagh, 1930-
  Ageism : negative and positive / Erdman B. Palmore.
    p.   cm.
  Includes bibliographical references.
  ISBN 0–8261–7000–5
  1. Ageism—United States. I. Title.
HQ1064.U5P258   1990
305.26'0973—cd20   90-9775
                                        CIP

Printed in the United States of America

Contents

v

Foreword

Historians continually remind us that the experience of aging is not what it was and not what it will be. In the colonial era, old age is said to have connoted honor and esteem. When ageism was decried by Robert Butler in 1975 in a pessimistic book about growing old in America entitled *Why Survive?*, old age was said to connote poverty, isolation, and illness. Sociologists have speculated about whether older people are properly classified as a minority group, who, like blacks or Hispanics, are subjects of prejudice and discrimination. This stereotype is quite distant from the newer imagery invoked in newspapers and national magazines in the late 1980s to pillory some opponents of the Catastrophic Health Care Act, which both began and ended in 1989, as comfortably rich and selfish. A national organization, AGE (Americans for Generation Equity), has argued that in America where the risk of impoverishment is greater for a child than for an older person, our prejudices favor older people and we discriminate against children.

Erdman Palmore has studied prejudice and discrimination toward older people in various ways throughout his long and distinguished career as a gerontologist. This book may be considered his final summation of the evidence and his current conclusions. His view is that simple stereotypes capture neither the variety of older adults in our society nor our responses to them. Older adults are rich and poor, wise and foolish, strong and weak, nice and mean. In a word, they are people who are older. Our prejudices toward them and our discrimination for or against them are too complex to manage with stereotypes.

In the 1980s the United States moved substantially toward becoming an age irrelevant society. Our notions about when one is old, should retire, change jobs, or have children, have become more complex. Age will probably never be totally irrelevant because it is too handy a bureaucratic and stereotypic convenience to organize our thoughts about whether people are on track and on time in their life course. The convenience of classifying people by chronological age can, however, be used while recognizing that age is not a real substitute for characterizing people in significant ways. Jean Paul Sartre once characterized *bad faith* as taking our stereotypes of people too seriously and treating our stereotypes as though they capture the essence of others.

Ageism is *bad faith*. Palmore has dedicated this book to suggesting there is a better, more accurate, and more useful way to think about later life and older adults. That way is to acknowledge that older adults age differently and appreciate that for the accomplishment that it is.

GEORGE L. MADDOX, PH.D.
Chair, Duke University Council on Aging
and Human Development

Preface

During my 26 years in gerontology, I have been fortunate to have had the time to write numerous articles and books on several different aspects of aging. But as I approach my own "golden years," I have begun to believe that there is one aspect of aging in our society that is more important than all the rest: ageism. Therefore, I believe this book is the most important thing I have ever written. I believe ageism (after racism and sexism) is emerging as the third great "ism" in our society, partly because it affects everyone, young and old, and partly because it involves basic questions of social policy as well as federal expenditures rivaling our military budget.

In this book I have tried to make a comprehensive review of the many different forms of ageism, including positive ageism, and to discuss the many methods that could be used to reduce ageism. I begin with a discussion of the meaning of ageism and its importance, then define the various types of ageism and related concepts, and review various conceptions of age. In Part II, I discuss the individual, social, and cultural influences on ageism, as well as the gains and costs of ageism. In Part III, I analyze the institutional patterns of ageism in the economy, government, family, housing, and health care. The last part discusses the relative effectiveness of various methods for reducing ageism, and speculates on the future of ageism. There are also appendices on the Facts of Aging Quizzes and ageism in humor.

I have tried to write in nontechnical language and to explain any jargon that was necessary, because I hope this book will be read by many nonprofessionals (as well as professionals) interested in the problems and opportunities of aging in our society. I have also documented the sources for the facts and theories I present so that the interested reader can pursue these ideas further. Thus, it should be useful as a text for students in gerontology.

When I was an undergraduate student at Duke University (class of '52), there was no teaching or research in gerontology on campus, much less any concern with ageism. But there was a growing concern with racism on our then segregated campus. This stimulated me to make race and ethnic relations one of my specialties within sociology. Later I became more and more aware that many of the principles of racism also apply to sexism.

About two decades ago, I became interested in how these principles apply to ageism, and published some research comparing racism, sexism, and ageism (Palmore & Manton, 1973). As I continued to teach race and ethnic relations, I became more impressed with how the standard texts in that field could be paralleled by a text on ageism. This book draws heavily on concepts, theories, and research dealing with racism and sexism.

This is the first comprehensive monograph on ageism. Barrow and Smith (1979) wrote the first book with ageism in its title, but it is now rather out of date, and deals more with society and aging in general than with ageism as such. Levin and Levin (1982) wrote a book entirely devoted to ageism, but it was relatively short (128 text pages) and dealt with only a few aspects of ageism. Neither book considered positive ageism. This book attempts to be both up to date and comprehensive.

Many people have contributed to this book, but I wish to especially thank my brother, Peyton L. Palmore III, D.Min., and my colleagues, Lucille Bearon, Ph.D. and Deborah Gold, Ph.D. for their careful reviews and useful suggestions. I also wish to thank my wife, Brydie, for her encouragement and for her continuing battle against sexism, which has sensitized me to those issues and to their parallels in ageism.

I also appreciate the kind foreword written by my distinguished colleague George Maddox, Ph.D. I owe him and Ewald Busse, M.D., a lifelong debt for bringing me to Duke University and making possible the research and writing I have enjoyed here for 23 years. Finally, I want to thank the Fulbright Commission and Harvey Cohen, M.D., Director of the Duke Center on Aging and

Human Development, for making available the time to research and write this book.

I would also be grateful to you dear reader, if you would send me your comments and suggestions for revision.

Part I
Concepts

1

Introduction and Basic Definitions

If a young or a middle-aged man, when leaving company, does not recollect where he had laid his hat, it is nothing; but if the same inattention is discovered in an old man, people will shrug their shoulders and say, "His memory is going."

Samuel Johnson

WHAT IS AGEISM?

Ageism has been called the ultimate prejudice, the last discrimination, the cruelest rejection. Edith Stein (unpublished) gives graphic examples of negative ageism:

Older persons falter for a moment because they are unsure of themselves and are immediately charged with being "infirm."

Older persons are constantly "protected" and their thoughts interpreted.

Older persons forget someone's name and are charged with senility and patronized.

Older persons are expected to "accept" the "facts of aging."

Older persons miss a word or fail to hear a sentence and they are charged with "getting old," not with a hearing difficulty.

Older persons are called "dirty" because they show sexual feeling or affection to one of either sex.

Older persons are called "cranky" when they are expressing a
legitimate distaste with life as so many young do.

Older persons are charged with being "like a child" even after
society has ensured that they are as dependent, helpless,
and powerless as children.

All societies use age and sex to classify their members and they
have different expectations for each category. But Americans have
developed a set of prejudices and discriminations against our elders that may be unequaled by any other society. The prejudices
range from the stereotype that most are senile to the cruel assumption that they have no need for sexual gratification. The discriminations range from forced retirement to elder abuse.

Racism became a burning issue in the 19th century and was
attacked by the abolitionist and civil rights movements. Sexism
became a burning issue in this century and was attacked by the
sufferage and equal-rights movements. Ageism is the third great
"ism" of our society. It is now being attacked by gerontologists and
the aged themselves.

Robert Butler, the first Director of the National Institute on
Aging, introduced the term "ageism" in 1969. He called it another
form of bigotry, similar to racism and sexism. He recently defined
it as "a process of systematic stereotyping and discrimination
against people because they are old" (p. 22, 1987). Webster's Dictionary (1984) now includes "ageism" and defines it as "prejudice
and discrimination against a particular age group, and especially
the elderly."

For the present book, ageism is defined as *any prejudice or discrimination against or in favor of an age group.* "Prejudice against
an age group" is a negative stereotype about that group (such as
the belief that most old people are senile), or a negative attitude
based on a stereotype (such as the feeling that old age is usually the
worst time of life). "Discrimination against an age group" is the
inappropriate negative treatment of members of that age group
(such as compulsory retirement).

The majority of Americans are prejudiced against elders in various ways. This is shown by the results of various studies which
have consistently found that the majority of those tested believe
the following erroneous stereotypes: many aged live in nursing
homes; the majority of aged are unable to adapt to change, are

bored, are lonely, live alone, live in poverty, are often irritated and angry; the aged have more injuries than younger persons, and the aged have higher rates of criminal victimization (Palmore, 1988). These and other common stereotypes are discussed further in Chapter 2 of the present book.

Ageism is reflected in such colloquialisms for elders as "coot," "crone," "geezer," "hag," "old buzzard," "old crock," "old duffer," "old fogey," "old goat," "old maid," "old-fangled," "old-fashioned," "out to pasture," "over the hill," and "washed up." Ageism is reinforced by the connotations of "old" such as "showing the effects of time or use—worn"; "no longer in use—discarded"; "antiquated or obsolete" (Webster's Dictionary, 1984). Chapter 6 discusses how ageism is reflected and reinforced by our language.

A major example of *discrimination* against elders is the policy of compulsory retirement for workers at age 65, regardless of their ability and health. This is an inappropriate differential treatment of those over 65 because most workers still employed at age 64 are quite capable of continuing their work beyond age 65 (see Chapter 8). There is no sudden or general loss of abilities at age 65 or at any other age. The losses that do occur tend to be gradual, affect some people only at extreme ages (90 and over), and some are reversible with proper treatment or may be compensated for with various devices (such as glasses or hearing aids).

On the other hand, some differential treatment of age groups is appropriate. For example, remaining life expectancy steadily declines with advancing age and so age is appropriately used to calculate the costs and benefits of life insurance policies and annuities at various ages. Similarly, speed and endurance of athletes tend to decline with age and so competition among older athletes tends to be age graded. That is, the athletes are grouped into age cohorts or categories so that members of each category compete only against each other rather than against younger or older persons.

Sometimes there is controversy as to whether a given differential treatment of an age group is appropriate or inappropriate; and which beliefs are true or false. Most beliefs about elders can be demonstrated to be true or false by the existing body of research in gerontology (Palmore, 1988). However, there are issues in gerontology that have not yet been resolved and there is room for debate as to which belief is more valid. For example, the extent to which genetics influence Alzheimer's disease and longevity is still controversial.

Furthermore, while there is now a broad consensus about most forms of age discrimination (as in the examples above), there is a lack of consensus on some issues and much debate about whether such actions are desirable or not. For example, is it wrong to force airline pilots to retire at a fixed age, or is it a prudent precaution against undetected declines in abilities or increased risk of sudden illness? For another example, is it wrong to give tax breaks to affluent elders just because of their age or is it a just reward for their years of service? We will be discussing such issues throughout the book, but especially in Part III.

The examples given so far are examples of prejudice and discrimination *against* the aged, or "negative ageism." But there is also "positive ageism": prejudice and discrimination *in favor* of the aged. For example, the provision of national health insurance (Medicare) for the aged but not the young is a form of ageism. For an example of positive prejudice, Binstock (1983) points out the new "tabloid thinking" which assumes that elders are well off and have been lifted out of poverty.

Previous books and articles on ageism neglect or ignore this kind of ageism (Barrow & Smith, 1979; Levin & Levin, 1980; Butler, 1969, 1975, 1987); but it is becoming as great a problem in recent years as negative ageism. Throughout this book, discussions of negative ageism will be balanced by discussions of positive ageism.

WHY IS AGEISM IMPORTANT?

Popular concern with ageism has been increasing rapidly in the last 10 years. Studies of mass media content have found that during the 1960s most of the space occupied by discrimination issues dealt with racism. Then by 1975 about half of the discrimination space dealt with racism and the other half with sexism. In 1977 both racism and sexism began to decline as the awareness of ageism increased, until the 1980s when ageism occupied about two-thirds of this space (Naisbitt, 1982).

Why has there been this rapid increase in concern with ageism? Perhaps the strongest factor has been the "aging of America." Most people are aware that the number of older people has been increasing rapidly and that it will continue to increase more rapidly than the rest of the population for many years to come (see Chapter 5). As their number increases so does concern with the problems of retirement and providing income security and medical care to such a large and vulnerable group. More recently their increasing number has caused concern about their growing and "disproportionate" political power (Binstock, 1983).

Concern over the unprecedented federal budget deficits has focused attention on the billions of dollars spent annually on income support, health, and welfare of elders. Many proposals have been made, and some have been adopted, to reduce the deficit by reducing the amounts of income support, medical care, and other services for the elderly. Such proposals have been bitterly resisted by the elderly and their organizations because they claim they are entitled to such programs. However, a growing number have begun to question this entitlement and argue that many such programs are a kind of reverse discrimination against younger people, or a kind of positive ageism (see Chapter 2).

Beyond the fact of increasing political concern with ageism, there are many personal consequences of ageism that make it an important ethical and social issue (see Chapter 7). There are the personal costs of demoralization, loss of self-esteem, loss of function, inactivity, physical and mental decline that can result from negative ageism.

Additionally, there are the economic costs of ignoring the productive and creative abilities of the millions of older people who are pressured to retire just because they are over 65. This waste will become more serious as the "baby bust" generation (with fewer members) enters the labor market and the number of younger workers declines.

Also there are the social and cultural costs of ignoring the wisdom and social support and cultural resources that are available from the millions of elders in our country. Most traditional societies still use these resources and many social problems of the industrialized societies (lack of adequate child care, juvenile delinquency, high crime rates, labor shortages, etc.) may be related to our neglect of these elder resources.

Finally, ageism is important because it violates basic democratic principles. The democratic ideal is that each person should be judged on the basis of individual merit rather than on the basis of group characteristics such as race, sex, and age. Furthermore, it is considered unethical, and usually illegal, to discriminate against a group because of these characteristics. Of course, these principles are often violated in practice, and there is much debate about which attitudes are prejudice and which behaviors are discrimination. But the principle is clear: prejudice and discrimination are undemocratic.

ARE THE AGED A MINORITY GROUP?

A generation ago Gordon Streib (1965), a distinguished social gerontologist, answered "No" to this question. On the other hand, several other distinguished gerontologists, such as Leonard Breen (1960), Milton Barron (1961), and Jack and William Levin (1980), have argued that the aged do have the main characteristics of minority groups.

Perhaps we can resolve this controversy by specifying what is usually meant by a "minority group" and then examining the evidence to see how well elders fit these criteria. Clearly, the fact that elders are a *statistical* minority has nothing to do with the issue. White Anglo-Saxon Protestant (WASP) males also are a statistical minority, but have none of the characteristics of minority groups. Conversely, women are a statistical majority, but are considered a minority group because of sexism.

The following five criteria are modified versions of Streib's criteria for minority groups (Palmore, 1978).

1. *Do elders have identifying characteristics with accompanying status-role expectations throughout the life cycle?* The answer is "yes" to the first part and "no" to the second. Yes, most persons over 65 possess the identifying characteristics of old age such as gray hair and wrinkles (unless they are chemically or surgically hidden); and there are accompanying status-role expectations such as retirement and increasing infirmity. But no, by definition, they do not possess this characteristic throughout life. The fact that they are not born with these characteristics makes their problems and opportunities rather different from those of the usual minority groups such as Blacks and women.

2. *Does the majority group hold negative stereotypes about elders?* Or, to put it more simply, is there prejudice against elders? The answer is clearly "yes." There are several common kinds of prejudice against the aged. Various studies have shown that the majority of Americans believe that most aged are sick or disabled, senile, impotent, useless, lonely, miserable, and in poverty (see Chapter 2).

3. *Are elders discriminated against?* The answer appears to be "no" in the area of most civil rights and political power; but in other areas such as employment, education, government services, and even in the family, the answer is "Yes" (see Part III).

4. *Are elders a deprived group?* Economically the aged are no

longer a deprived group (see Chapter 8). They now have *less* poverty than those under 65, and have a greater proportion of the national personal income than their proportion in the population. Also there is little residential or institutional segregation of the kind encountered by racial minorities. The main area in which they could be considered deprived is the area of employment; despite laws to the contrary, many are pressured or forced to retire even though they are willing and able to keep working.

5. *Do elders have a sense of group identity or political unity?* The answer appears to be "Some do, but the majority don't." The majority deny that there is *any* chronologic dividing line marking the beginning of old age (Harris, 1981). They tend to use functional criteria to identify old age, such as retirement or poor health. Many are ashamed of their age and the majority resist identification as old or elderly (see Chapter 7). Elders are at least as heterogeneous in their attitudes, behaviors, and politics as are younger people. There is little or no "aged vote" (see Chapter 9).

On the other hand, there are substantial numbers who are developing a sense of group identity and who join special organizations for elders. The American Association of Retired Persons and the National Retired Teachers Association now have a combined membership of about 30 million. They and other groups such as the National Council of Senior Citizens and the National Council on the Aging engage in lobbying and political pressure for elders. However, their main success appears to be in the area of maintaining Social Security benefits and funding for the Administration on Aging.

So the question, "Are the aged a minority group?" cannot be answered simply "yes" or "no." In some respects they resemble the traditional minority groups and in other respects they are clearly different. They do suffer from prejudice and discrimination, but they are not born into the group and the majority do not have much sense of group identity or political unity. Barron's (1961) term, "quasi-minority group," would be the best description of elders today.

RACISM, SEXISM, AND AGEISM

How does ageism compare with the other two major "ism's" in our society? Which is stronger in our society: race, sex, or age inequality? Civil rights leaders assert that racism results in the most serious inequality, while feminist leaders assert that sexism is a more serious problem. More recently some gerontologists have argued that ageism is becoming at least as important as racism and sexism (Levin & Levin, 1980; Naisbitt, 1982).

However, there have been few attempts to compare quantitatively the relative importance of these three kinds of prejudice and discrimination. We (Palmore & Manton, 1973) have analyzed the race, sex, and age inequalities shown by the U.S. census statistics using the method of the "Equality Index." We compared inequalities in terms of income, education, occupation, and number of weeks worked. The "Equality Index" summarizes the amount of similarity (or equality) between the percentage distributions of two groups, such as the aged and nonaged, on a given dimension, such as income or years of education.

We found that age inequality was greater than race and sex inequality in the number of years of education completed and in the number of weeks worked; that is, there was more discrepancy between the aged and nonaged in their education and weeks worked, than there was between the whites and nonwhites, and between males and females. However, in terms of occupation, age inequality was less than racial and sex inequality. Age inequality was also greater than racial inequality in terms of income (although this statistic has probably changed since 1973).

When comparisons were made combining two of the factors, the joint effects were generally additive. The combination of all three factors produced the lowest equality in both income and occupation. Changes since 1950 show nonwhites and the aged gaining substantially more equality in income, occupation, and education; while women were barely maintaining their generally inferior status (Palmore, 1976).

The extent to which these inequalities are directly due to racism, sexism, and ageism, as opposed to biological or cohort differences, is difficult to determine. However, it is clear that the relative amounts of race, sex, and age inequality vary depending on which inequality is being measured.

COHORT CHANGES

Elders have been gaining on younger people not only in terms of income, occupation, and education, but also in health (Palmore,

1986). Our analysis of data from the Health Interview Survey since 1961 found that all measures of illness and disability showed decreasing disability for successive cohorts of people 65 and over relative to younger persons.

Are these gains due primarily to reductions in ageism, to improved support and services for elders, or to cohort changes? They are probably due to a combination of these factors, but primarily to cohort changes.

What are cohort changes? For our purposes, a cohort is a category of people born during a certain period. For example, the cohort of people born between 1920 and 1930 will be 60 to 70 years old in 1990. They are a more affluent, better educated, and healthier cohort than cohorts born before 1920. This is because the newer cohorts had more fortunate life experiences. They had more education as youth; did not suffer from loss of savings and unemployment during the Depression; and had better nutrition, sanitation, and health care throughout their lives.

Thus, as the newer cohorts replace the older cohorts among those over 65, the average income, education, and health of elders improves. This is the primary explanation for the improvement in characteristics of elders.

FROM NEGATIVE TO POSITIVE AGEISM

There is some evidence that these improvements in the characteristics of elders have resulted in more positive views of aging (Austin, 1985). Tibbitts (1979) claimed that during the past 30 to 40 years, U.S. society has moved from holding negative stereotypes of old people to holding positive views in which elders are seen as being able to contribute to the quality of life for themselves, their communities, and society as a whole. Schonfield (1982) even argued that the assumption of negative attitudes toward old people is a "social myth" perpetuated by the gerontological literature. We will be examining these attitudes in detail in Chapter 2, but there does appear to be a substantial shift from negative to positive attitudes.

The improvements in the physical, mental, social, and economic characteristics of elders have been so marked, and there have been so many programs and services developed for elders only, that many have begun to criticize these programs as discrimination *in favor* of the aged, or positive ageism. We will be discussing ex-

amples of positive ageism throughout this book; but the ones that
have drawn most criticism so far are the Medicare program (Chapter 11) and some features of the Social Security System, such as
the automatic cost of living increases in benefits and the tax-exemption of Social Security benefits for most elders (Chapter 8).
Perhaps these programs have been criticized the most because
they involve the most money.

Critics are beginning to argue that since elders are no longer
deprived economically (as a group) and since they are now much
better off mentally, physically, and socially than they were in the
past, it is no longer necessary or fair to continue the enormous
expense of these special supports and programs available only to
elders (Neugarten, 1982; Kutza, 1981). Some argue that the way to
reduce positive ageism is to make these supports and programs
available to all ages on the basis of need. For example, they recommend that the national health insurance (Medicare), which only
elders now enjoy, be extended to all ages (see Chapter 14).

It is clear that positive ageism is becoming an important issue
and promises to become even more important as we are faced with
more older people and more expensive programs for "seniors
only."

SENESCENCE AND SENILITY

Senescence, according to the dictionary, simply means the process
or condition of "growing old" (Webster, 1984). However, to biologists and psychologists it connotes "those manifestations in structure and function of a declining or deteriorating nature which take
place during the period of life when the mortality rate of a population is accelerated" (Finch & Hayflick, 1977, p. 5). It also implies
progressive and irreversible deterioration. Thus, the connotations
are entirely negative. It ignores all the recovery, restoration,
growth, development, and improvement of abilities that are possible as humans age.

The assumption that senescence or deterioration is all there is to
human aging is a negative form of ageism. On the other hand, to
deny the senescence or declines in function that usually accompany aging is a positive form of ageism.

Senility is defined as "the physical and mental infirmity of old
age" (Webster, 1984). It is not actually a medical or scientific term,

but it is often used by doctors and laypeople alike to "explain" the behavior and condition of older people. Many of the reactive emotional responses of older people, such as depression, grief, and anxiety, are labeled senility and mistakenly considered to be irreversible and untreatable (Butler & Lewis, 1982). This is another form of ageism.

Actual brain damage from cerebral arteriosclerosis or Alzheimer's disease probably accounts for only about half of the mental disorders in old age (Butler & Lewis, 1982). Only 5 to 10 percent of those over 65 have mental disorders severe enough to interfere with normal function (Busse & Blazer, 1980).

GERONTOLOGY AND GERIATRICS

Gerontology is defined as the science of aging. Actually it is made up of the knowledge about aging derived from many sciences, including biology, psychology, and sociology. Gerontologists are the scientists who study aging.

Gerontologists have been accused of focusing only on the declines of aging (senescence), and of assuming that the characteristics of the aged are the primary causes of the problems of elders (Levin & Levin, 1980). Such a focus on declines is a subtle form of ageism because it ignores the possibilities of growth and improvement with age. The assumption that the characteristics of elders are the cause of the problems of elders is another subtle form of ageism, because it ignores the extent to which the ageism embedded in our social structure and culture contribute to the problems of elders (see Chapters 5 and 6).

The extent to which various theories in gerontology may contribute to ageism is discussed in Chapter 6.

Geriatrics is the study of the medical aspects of old age, and the application of gerontology to the prevention, diagnosis, and treatment of illness among older persons (Butler, 1987a). Thus, while gerontology deals with all aspects of aging, geriatrics is limited to the medical aspects.

Physicians may be subject to several kinds of ageism (Chapter 11). Because they focus on illness and disability, they may forget that health and ability is normal among elders. They may be tempted to blame any difficult or obscure illness on old age and assume that nothing can be done about it.

Geriatricians and other providers of service to elders may ex-
aggerate age differences and needs of elders in order to promote
their own service roles (Estes, 1979). Several gerontologists charge
that gerontology is becoming increasingly "biomedicalized" and
that this produces a negative view of aging (Estes & Binney, 1989).

Kalish (1979) suggested that there is a "new ageism" found
especially among advocates and service providers for the aged:

1. It stereotypes the "elderly" in terms of the characteristics of
   the least capable, least healthy, and least alert of the elderly.
2. It perceives the older person as, in effect, a relatively helpless
   and dependent individual who requires the support services
   of agencies and other organizations.
3. It encourages the development of services without adequate
   concern as to whether the outcome of these services contributes to reduction of freedom for the participants to make
   decisions controlling their own lives.
4. It produces an unrelenting stream of criticism against society
   in general and certain individuals in society for the mistreat-
   ment of the elderly, emphasizing the unpleasant existence
   faced by the elderly.

AGE STRATIFICATION, AGE NORMS, AND AGE CONFLICT

Age stratification is the system that classifies people by their age
(Riley, 1987). All societies stratify their members by age (as well as
by sex and socioeconomic status, and often by race). In all these
stratification systems, there is an implicit or explicit ranking from
higher to lower strata.

In gerontocratic societies, the old have the highest status and the
youngest have the lowest. In our society, the middle-aged tend to
have the most power and prestige, while children have the least.
The old and the young tend to be in between, and whether the old
or the young are higher than the other depends on which dimension is involved. In terms of income elders tend to rank higher than
the young. In terms of sports and entertainment the young tend to
rank higher.

Such ranking of individuals on the basis of their age is a form of
ageism that accompanies age stratification systems.

Age norms are the expectations about the proper or normal behaviors, obligations, and privileges for the age strata or life stages (Back, 1987). For example, children are expected to go to school, have the obligation to obey parents, and the privilege of being supported by their parents. In contrast, elders are expected to retire, have the obligation to take care of their health and assets, and the privilege of being supported by Social Security benefits.

The extent to which such age norms are ageism depends on whether the assumptions on which they are based are prejudicial or not; and whether the expectations are realistic and appropriate or not.

Age conflict is an extreme form of ageism in which two or more age strata conflict with each other (Foner, 1987). Some age conflict probably occurs in all societies and may be an inevitable result of their age stratification. Like other forms of social conflict, age conflicts involve struggles over scarce resources or over values. Age inequalities are a major source of age conflicts (Foner, 1974; Lenski, 1966). Struggles occur when the disadvantaged age group make claims for more power or other goods while the more advantaged seek to protect their privileges.

However, such conflicts tend to be confined to particular institutions like the family or the workplace, rather than becoming societywide. There are many factors that tend to check sharp age conflicts, such as the legitimation of age inequalities by various stereotypes, the fear of painful consequences from those in power, ties of affection or obligation, and social separation of age groups.

The amount of age conflict in our society has sometimes been exaggerated. There is little disagreement between the generations about the Social Security system or other programs for elders. Similarly, there is general agreement between generations about our basic value system. There is little difference between generations in voting behavior.

SUMMARY

Ageism is prejudice or discrimination against or in favor of an age group. Prejudice against an age group is a negative stereotype or negative attitude toward that group. Discrimination against an age group is the negative treatment of members of that group.

The majority of Americans are prejudiced against elders in various ways as shown by their belief in many negative stereotypes and their use of ageist language. Compulsory retirement at age 65 is a common example of discrimination against elders. On the other hand, some differential treatment of age groups is appropriate, such as differential premiums for life insurance by age groups.

Ageism is an increasingly important issue because of the rapidly increasing numbers of older people; the Federal budget deficits; the personal, economic, social, and cultural costs of ageism. Ageism also violates basic democratic principles.

Elders are like minority groups in that they have identifying characteristics with accompanying status-role expectations, they suffer from prejudice and discrimination, and some have a sense of group identity. They are different from other minority groups in that they do not belong to this group during most of their lives, and they are no longer an economically deprived group.

Age inequality is greater than race and sex inequality in terms of years of education completed and number of weeks worked. Changes since 1950 show elders and nonwhites making substantial gains in income, occupation, and education; while women were hardly improving their generally inferior financial and occupational status. Cohort changes are the main explanations for the gains of elders relative to younger people.

Elders have made such substantial gains in status that many critics have begun to argue that many of the programs and services "for seniors only" have become positive ageism. Certainly this is an issue that will increase in importance as the costs of these programs increase.

Senescence connotes decline and deterioration in biological structures or functions with aging. To emphasize senescence without recognizing the growth, recovery, and improvement that occurs in old age is a form of negative ageism. Senility refers to the mental infirmities of old age. It is not a useful medical term and its use to "explain" all the problems of elders is another form of ageism.

Gerontology is the science of aging, while geriatrics is the medical application of gerontology to the prevention, diagnosis, and treatment of illness among elders. Gerontologists and geriatricians may be subject to several forms of ageism.

Age stratification is the system that stratifies or ranks people by their age. The ranking of people because of their age is a form of ageism. Age norms are the expectations about the proper behaviors, obligations, and privileges of the age strata. When these norms are based on prejudicial assumptions, they are a form of ageism. Age conflict is an extreme form of ageism in which two or more age strata conflict with each other. Age inequalities are a major source of conflict. Insofar as such conflict is based on age differences, it is a form of ageism.

We now turn to a discussion of various types of negative and positive ageism.

2
Types of Ageism

Getting old is exactly like having a criminal record. From now on, every little thing counts against you.

Marie Baird, 1986

Prejudice against elders can be divided into negative stereotypes and negative attitudes. Stereotypes are mistaken or exaggerated beliefs about a group, in this case the elderly. Negative attitudes are negative feelings about a group. Stereotypes are more cognitive while attitudes are more affective, although both tend to go together. Negative stereotypes usually produce negative attitudes and negative attitudes support negative stereotypes (see Figure 2.1).

NEGATIVE STEREOTYPES

There are at least nine major stereotypes that reflect negative prejudice toward elders: illness, impotency, ugliness, mental decline, mental illness, uselessness, isolation, poverty, and depression. For each stereotype, we will first review the evidence for the frequency of the stereotype and then the facts about its validity.

1. *Illness.* Perhaps the most common prejudice against elders is that most are sick or disabled. About half of Americans think that

	NEGATIVE		POSITIVE	
PREJUDICE	Stereotypes	Attitudes	Stereotypes	Attitudes
DISCRIMINATION	Personal	Institutional	Personal	Institutional

Figure 2.1 Types of Ageism

poor health is a "very serious problem" for most people over 65 (Harris, 1981). Earlier surveys found that from one-fifth to two-thirds of various groups agree with the following statements: older people "spend much time in bed because of illness"; "have many accidents in the home"; "have poor coordination"; "feel tired most of the time"; and "develop infection easily" (Tuckman & Lorge, 1958). Studies using the Facts on Aging Quizzes (FAQ) have usually found that a majority mistakenly believe that large proportions of elders are confined to long-stay institutions; and that older people have more injuries in the home than younger people (Palmore, 1988). Also many mistakenly believe that elders have more acute illness than younger people and that the majority of elders are not healthy enough to carry out their normal activities.

FACTS: Most elders (about 78% of those 65+) are healthy enough to engage in their normal activities (National Center for Health Statistics, 1981). Only 5 percent of those 65 and over are institutionalized and about 81 percent of the noninstitutionalized have no limitation in their activities of daily living: eating, bathing, dressing, toileting, and so on. (Soldo & Manton, 1983).

While more persons over 65 have chronic illnesses that limit their activity (43%) than do younger persons (10%), elders actually have fewer acute illnesses than do younger persons (102 acute illnesses per 100 persons over 65 per year, compared to 230 for persons under 65: National Center for Health Statistics, 1978). Furthermore, elders have fewer injuries in the home (12.5 per person over 65 compared to 14 per person under 65: National

Center for Health Statistics, 1978), and fewer accidents on the highway than younger persons (National Safety Council, 1981). Thus, the higher rate of chronic illness among elders is offset by the lower rates of acute illness, injury, and accidents.

These lower rates are probably due mainly to the fact that elders usually take better care of themselves: they avoid the exposure to infectious deseases that occurs at schools and workplace; and they avoid the dangerous situations that cause injuries and accidents.

In addition there is evidence that disability is *decreasing* among elders (Palmore, 1986; Crimmins, Saito, & Ingegneri, 1989).

2. *Impotency*. A related stereotype is the belief that most elders no longer have any sexual activity or even sexual desire, and that those few who do are morally perverse or at least abnormal (Golde & Kogan, 1959; Cameron, 1970). Even physicians, who should know better, often assume that sexuality is unimportant in late life (Butler, 1975). Many jokes and birthday cards are based on this belief (see Chapter 6). The fact that many older people believe this stereotype makes them ashamed of their sexual urges and may prevent their enjoyment of normal sexual activity (Williamson, Evans, & Nunley, 1980). It may also prevent remarriage of widows and widowers in late life (see Chapter 10).

FACTS: The majority of persons past 65 continue to have both interest and capacity for sexual relations. Masters and Johnson (1966) found that the capacity for satisfying sexual relations usually continues into the seventies and eighties for healthy couples. The Duke Longitudinal Studies (Palmore, 1981) found that sex continues to play an important role in the lives of the majority of men and women through the seventh decade of life.

A large-scale survey (Starr & Weiner, 1981) found that most elders said that sex after 60 was as satisfying or *more* satisfying than when younger. Reasons given for more satisfying sexual relations included no fear of pregnancy, less stress from job and child-rearing responsibilities, more leisure time, and more mature relationships.

3. *Ugliness*. Another related stereotype is that old people are ugly. A study using drawings of attractive and unattractive faces found that among both younger (under 30) and older (over 56) persons, there was a strong association between perceptions of older age and unattractiveness (Wernick & Manaster, 1984). Beauty is usually associated with youth, and many people, especially women, fear the loss of their beauty as they age. The following terms for old people reflect the stereotype of ugliness: crone, fossil, goat, hag, witch, withered, wizened, wrinkled.

FACTS: While our culture tends to associate old age with ugliness, and youth with beauty, some other cultures tend to admire the characteristics of old age. For example in Japan, silver hair and wrinkles are often admired as signs of wisdom, maturity, and long years of service (Palmore, 1985).

Thus, there is nothing inherently ugly or repelling about the characteristics of old age. Ugliness is a subjective value judgment, or, in other words, "ugliness is in the eye of the beholder." These value judgments usually conform to cultural standards of beauty and ugliness.

4. *Mental Decline.* Another common stereotype is that mental abilities begin to decline from middle age onward (or even earlier), especially the abilities to learn and remember. The well-known aphorism "You can't teach an old dog new tricks" sums up this stereotype. Various studies using the Facts on Aging Quizzes have found substantial numbers of people who believe "It is almost impossible for the average old person to learn something new," and "Cognitive impairment (memory loss, disorientation, or confusion) is an inevitable part of the aging process" (Palmore, 1988).

FACTS: Most elders retain their normal mental abilities, including the ability to learn and remember. It is true that reaction time tends to slow down in old age and it may take somewhat longer to learn something. However, much of these differences between older and younger persons can be explained by variables other than age (illness, motivation, learning style, lack of practice, amount of education). When these other variables are taken into account, chronological age does not provide a significant amount of influence on learning ability (Poon, 1987).

Most studies of short-term memory agree that there is little or no decline in everyday short-term memory among normal elders (Kausler, 1987). As for long-term memory, various community surveys have found that less than 20 percent of elders cannot remember such things as the past President of the United States; their correct age, birth date, telephone number, mother's maiden name, or address; or the meaning of ordinary words (Botwinick, 1967; Pfeiffer, 1975). Thus, it is clear that while there may be some increase in long-term memory problems, the majority do not have serious memory defects.

5. *Mental Illness.* A similar stereotype is that many or most aged are "senile" and that mental illness is common, inevitable, and untreatable among most aged. Two-thirds of those surveyed think that elders have more mental impairments than younger people, and some even believe that the majority of persons over 65 have

some mental illness severe enough to impair their abilities (Palmore, 1988). This belief is particularly vicious because it can become a self-fulfilling prophecy in which the belief that mental illness is inevitable and untreatable leads to lack of prevention and treatment, which in turn tends to confirm the original belief. This helps explain why elders use mental health facilities at only one-half the rate of the general population (Lebowitz, 1987). Both elders themselves and many health professionals think that most mental illness in old age is untreatable.

FACTS: Most elders are not senile and mental illness is neither common, inevitable, nor untreatable. Only about 2 percent of persons 65 and over are institutionalized with a primary diagnosis of psychiatric illness (George, 1984). All community studies of psychopathology among elders agree that less than 10 percent have significant or severe mental illness, and another 10 to 32 percent have mild to moderate mental impairment; but that the majority are without impairment (Blazer, 1980). In fact, according to the most comprehensive and careful community surveys, *fewer* of the elderly have mental impairments than do younger persons (Myers, Weissman, Tischler, Hozer, & Leaf, 1984).

6. *Uselessness.* Because of these beliefs that the majority of old people are disabled by physical or mental illness, many people conclude that the elderly are unable to continue working and that those few who do continue to work are unproductive. Over a third of college students think "Older workers usually cannot work as effectively as younger workers" (Palmore, 1977). This belief is the main basis for compulsory retirement policies and discrimination in hiring, retraining, and promotion.

FACTS: The majority of older workers can work as effectively as younger workers. Studies of employed older people under actual working conditions generally show that they perform as well as, if not better than, younger workers on most measures (Krauss, 1987; Riley & Foner, 1968). When speed and accuracy of movement are important to the job, some studies indicate some decline with age (Rhodes, 1983). However, intellectual performance, on which much of work performance depends, does not decline substantially until the seventies in most individuals and even later in others (Labouvie-Vief, 1985). Consistency of output tends to increase with age, and older workers have less job turnover, fewer accidents, and less absenteeism than younger workers (Riley & Foner, 1968).

Over three-fourths of people over 65 are doing useful work or would like to have some work to do. About 11 percent are in the labor force, 21 percent are retired but say they would like to be employed, 17 percent work as homemakers, 19 percent are not employed but do volunteer work, and another 9 percent would like to do volunteer work (Harris, 1975, 1981).

7. *Isolation.* From a third to half of respondents to the Facts on Aging Quiz think "The majority of old people are socially isolated and lonely" and "The majority of old people live alone" (Palmore, 1988). Two-thirds of persons under 65 think that loneliness is a "very serious problem" for most people over 65 (Harris, 1981).

FACTS: The majority of elders are not socially isolated. About two-thirds live with their spouse or family (U.S. Senate Special Committee on Aging, 1988). Only about 4 percent of elders are extremely isolated, and most of these have had lifelong histories of withdrawal (B. Kahana, 1987). Most elders have close relatives within easy visiting distance, and contacts between them are relatively frequent.

Most studies agree that there tends to be a decline in total social activity with age, but the total number of persons in the social network tends to remain steady (Palmore, 1981). The types of persons in the social network tend to shift from older to younger persons, and from friends and neighbors to children and other relatives.

8. *Poverty.* Views about the economic status of elders range from those who think most elders are poor, to those who think the majority are rich. At present those thinking elders are poor tend to outnumber those thinking elders are rich. Over half of respondents to the Facts on Aging Quiz think "The majority of old people have incomes below the poverty line" (Palmore, 1988). More than 80 percent mistakenly believe "The aged do not get their proportionate share of the nation's income." Over two-thirds of people under 65 believe "not having enough money to live on" is a "very serious problem" for most people over 65 (Harris, 1981).

FACTS: Most elders have incomes well above the federal poverty level (U.S.Senate Special Committee on Aging, 1988). In 1986 only 12.4 percent had incomes below the poverty level ($5,255 for an aged individual or $6,630 for an aged couple). This was a lower poverty rate than for persons under 65 (13.7%). Even if the "near poor" (those with incomes up to 150% of the poverty level) are included, the total in or near poverty was only 28 percent.

Furthermore, the average elder is somewhat more affluent than the average person under 65. For example, in 1983 the mean per capita family income before taxes of households headed by a person over age 65 was $9,080, while that for households with a head aged 25 to 64 was $8,960 (Schick, 1986). When differences in taxes and noncash benefits (such as Medicare) are taken into account, it can be argued that elders receive *more* than their proportionate share of the national personal income (Fried, Rivlin, Schultze, & Teeters, 1973).

For another example, a higher proportion of elders than the total population have a net worth of over $50,000 (25% of elders versus 19% of all individuals have net worth of $50,000 to $100,000: Chen, 1988).

9. *Depression.* Since many believe that the typical older person is sick, impotent, senile, useless, lonely, and in poverty, they naturally conclude that the typical older person must also be miserable. Common terms for older people are "grouchy," "touchy," "cranky," and "feel sorry for themselves." A third of respondents to the Facts on Aging and Mental Health Quiz believe "Major depression is more prevalent among the elderly than among younger persons" and about a tenth even believe "The majority of old people feel miserable most of the time" (Palmore, 1988).

A recent study of responses to a series of old and young faces with neutral or relaxed expressions found that compared to the young faces, old faces were significantly more likely to be interpreted as sad or depressed (Fredrickson, Collins, & Carstensen, 1989). Since people expect elders to be sad, they mistakenly interpret neutral expressions as sad ones.

FACTS: Major depression is *less* prevalent among the elderly than among younger persons. The NIMH survey of three communities found that major depressive disorders (not counting bereavement) were less than half as prevalent among those over 65 as in the general population (Myers et al, 1984). Bereavement was more common in the oldest age group among women, but not among men.

Furthermore, the majority of elders are relatively happy most of the time. Studies of happiness, morale, and life satisfaction either find no significant difference by age group or find about one-fifth to one-third of elders score "low" on various happiness or morale scales (Larson, 1978; Palmore, 1981). A nationwide survey found only one-fourth of elders reporting that "This is the dreariest time of my life," while about half said, "I am just as happy as when I was younger," and one-third even said, "These are the best years of my life" (Harris, 1981).

A CAUTION. We should recognize that most people believe only some of these stereotypes and some people do not believe any of them (Schonfield, 1982; Palmore, 1988). Furthermore, when given the opportunity to recognize exceptions to these stereotypes, 80 percent or more of respondents recognize that there are numerous exceptions (Schonfield, 1982). Thus, few believe that all aged fit any one of these stereotypes.

NEGATIVE ATTITUDES

What about overall feelings toward old age? Do most people like or dislike old age? Which ages do they prefer?

The most definitive answers to these questions come from the nationally representative survey carried out by Louis Harris for the National Council on the Aging (1975). They asked people of all ages, "What do you think are the best years of a person's life?" Among those under 65, only one percent said the sixties or seventies. Even among those who have reached the later years themselves (that is, over 65) only eight percent said the sixties or seventies! The most frequently chosen "best years" were the twenties and thirties (chosen by a majority of the total).

Similarly, when asked "What are the worst years of a person's life?" about half of those specifying the "worst years" chose the sixties or seventies. The other half tended to pick the teens or the twenties as the worst years.

As for why people chose the older years as the "worst years," over two-thirds said "bad health," "illness," or some other term for physical decline. In contrast, senility or mental decline was cited by only a few (3%). The second most frequent reason for chosing the older years as the "worst years" was financial problems, cited by about one-fifth.

When asked to volunteer what are "the worst things about being over 65 years of age," again about two-thirds said poor health or physical condition. The second most frequent category was loneliness, volunteered by one-third. Financial problems were volunteered by one-fifth.

Another indication from this survey of negative attitudes toward old age is the fact that people of all ages evaluated the problems of older people to be much more frequent than they actually were among the older respondents. Furthermore, this misperception did not decline between the first survey (1974) and the second (1981) (Ferraro, 1989).

Even children tend to have negative attitudes toward the elderly. For example, Seefeldt, Jantz, Galper, & Serock (1977) found that 60 percent of schoolchildren preferred to be with the youngest man (in a series of drawings) and only 20 percent preferred to be with the oldest. This finding is consistent with most of the other studies in this area, although children usually have mixtures of negative and positive stereotypes about the elderly. (Hickey, Hickey, & Kalish, 1968; Hickey & Kalish, 1968; Thomas & Yamamoto, 1975).

McTavish, in a review of the literature (1971), concluded that between a fifth and a third of adults in the United States agree with negative statements about older people. Most people have mixtures of negative and some positive attitudes toward elders. However, it appears that very few, even among those over 65, have predominantly positive attitudes toward old age; while substantial proportions have predominantly negative attitudes (Palmore, 1982).

The most common reason for the negative attitudes is the first stereotype cited above: illness. No other stereotype is nearly as important. This conclusion is supported by several studies (Harris, 1975; Palmore, 1982).

One experiment found that just the sound of an older person's voice can trigger negative attitudes. Undergraduate college students listened to tapes of younger (20–22) and older (60–65) male speakers reading identical material, and rated the speakers on various dimensions. The older speakers were rated as significantly less competent, less flexible, more old-fashioned, and from lower social classes (Stewart & Ryan, 1982).

NEGATIVE DISCRIMINATION

If people kept their negative prejudices to themselves, no harm would come from them. Unfortunately, prejudice usually results in discrimination. Discrimination against elders occurs in five major institutions in our society: employment, government agencies, family, housing, and health care.

1. *Employment.* Perhaps the most obvious and serious form of discrimination is in the area of employment: from hiring and promotions to firing and compulsory retirement (see Chapter 8). Despite federal legislation against discrimination in employment

because of age, most observers agree that it continues to be a common practice. The 1971 and 1981 Harris surveys both found that 8 out of 10 Americans believe that "most employers discriminate against older people and make it difficult for them to find work." This perception is also shared by a majority of business leaders: 6 out of 10 employers believe older workers today are discriminated against in the employment marketplace (U.S. Senate Special Committee on Aging, 1986).

Another indication of the extent of this discrimination is the frequency of legal suits charging age discrimination in employment. For example, in 1986 the Equal Employment Opportunity Commission filed 118 lawsuits under the Age Discrimination in Employment Act (U.S. Senate Special Committee on Aging, 1986).

2. *Government Agencies.* One might think that because of the various laws passed by Congress against age discrimination, the government would be one place free of such discrimination (see Chapter 9). However, the U.S. Commission on Civil Rights (1977) found that age discrimination was present in each of 10 federal programs. Community mental health centers, legal services, vocational rehabilitation, social services to low-income individuals and families, employment and training services, the Food Stamp program, Medicaid, and vocational education all tended to discriminate against older people in various ways. Furthermore, this discrimination was common in all regions of the country and against all of the older age groups, although the oldest age groups (75+) tended to experience more discrimination.

For example, community mental health centers generally interpret "preventive health care" as applying only to children and adolescents, so older adults get little or no preventive care. Directors of employment programs tend to focus their efforts on males aged 22 to 44.

Furthermore, states and local governments discriminate against older persons by defining younger persons as the only ones eligible for federal programs. For example, several states exclude older people from vocational rehabilitation programs because they are not of "employable age."

3. *Family.* One might think that in the bosom of the family older relatives would be free from discrimination. It probably is true that there is less discrimination in the family against older persons than in other areas. Unfortunately, however, there is considerable evidence now that many families discriminate against their older members in various ways (see Chapter 10).

Elder abuse and neglect is the most extreme form of such discrimination. The U.S. House Select Committee on Aging (1981) estimated that four percent of older people are abused every year. In addition, some older family members are ignored, disparaged, restricted unnecessarily, or sent to long-term care institutions before it is necessary. We have already noted how most children tend to prefer to be with younger rather than older people (Seefeldt et al., 1977)

4. *Housing*. More and more elders are concentrated in certain states, counties, sections of cities, and in special residences for elders (Golant, 1975). There are high concentrations of elders in California, Arizona, and Florida. The urban aged are concentrated in the central city and the rural aged are concentrated in villages (U.S. Bureau of Census, 1984a).

The question that cannot be answered at present is how much of this concentration is voluntary and how much is overtly or covertly forced on elders by others. Overt age discrimination in housing by real estate agents, lenders, or sellers is now illegal. It is probable that most aged living in age-segregated housing prefer that type of housing. Most residents of retirement communities say it is easier to make friends there than in age-integrated communities, and they have higher morale than those in normal communities (Bultena & Wood, 1969).

However, the pervasive ageism in our society may be an indirect cause of this age segregation: older people may make friends easier and may be happier in age-segregated communities because they do not have to face the ageism common among younger people (see Chapter 11).

5. *Health Care*. It is difficult to assess the adequacy of medical care for elders (Chapter 11). On the one hand, elders are the only age group covered by national health insurance (Medicare), and they certainly consume disproportionately large amounts of medical care. On the other hand, there are several indications that they still receive less adequate care than other age groups.

First, the widespread belief (often shared by elders themselves) that most of the illnesses and health conditions of older people are "normal" and irreversible, prevents the adequate treatment of many illnesses that are in fact reversible. Second, there is extensive evidence that most health professionals are prejudiced against elders and prefer to treat children or young adults (Palmore, 1988; Quinn, 1987a). Third, despite Medicare, there are still formidable barriers to adequate care, including financial and transportation barriers, ignorance, and denial among elders (Palmore, 1972a). Fourth, despite the fact that elders have higher rates of health services consumption, these rates are still lower than might be expected on the basis of their much higher rates of illness and chronic conditions (Palmore, 1972a). It is probable that many elders would get more adequate health care if they were younger.

A recent best seller has proposed that old age be used as an explicit criteria to limit health care for chronically ill patients (Callahan, 1987). This is an extreme form of discrimination in health care (see Chapter 11).

POSITIVE STEREOTYPES

Much less attention has been paid to positive ageism than to negative ageism for several reasons: positive ageism is less common, and it is less harmful to elders. Nevertheless, there are many positive stereotypes about elders and some people who have generally positive attitudes toward elders.

There are at least eight major positive stereotypes that many people believe: kindness, wisdom, dependability, affluence, political power, freedom, eternal youth, and happiness. Notice that many of these positive stereotypes are the opposite of corresponding negative stereotypes discussed previously.

1. *Kindness.* This stereotype provides the image of the kindly grandmother or grandfather, spoiling their grandchildren, helping to support their children, and being kind and generous to people in general, but especially to children. This is one of the most common stereotypes as shown by several studies (Axelrod & Eisdorfer, 1961; Braithwaite, 1986; Thomas & Yamamoto, 1975; Tuckman & Lorge, 1953). Three-fourths of Americans think most people over 65 are "very friendly and warm" (Harris, 1975).

Facts. There is no direct evidence on this stereotype, but the indirect evidence tends to contradict it. If elders were kinder people, one might expect that they would spend more time caring for members of the family, socializing with friends, and doing volunteer work. In fact, fewer elders compared to those under 65 say they spend "a lot of time" caring for members of the family (20% compared to 50%); and fewer aged say they spend "a lot of time" socializing with friends (38% compared to 45%). Only 8 percent of elders say they spend "a lot of time" doing volunteer work (Harris, 1975).

If elders were kinder people one might also expect that their attitudes would be more "liberal," that is, they would be more permissive toward human behavior, they would favor social change to improve society, they would deemphasize authority and obedience, they would favor more foreign aid and less military spending.

In fact, public opinion polls tend to contradict this stereotype. Campbell and Strate (1981) made a comprehensive analysis of the responses of persons 65 and over compared to those of persons 30 to 64 on these issues in the 14 American National Election Studies conducted between 1952 and 1980. They found that *fewer* elders than younger adults were liberal on most of these issues; similar proportions of elders and younger adults were liberal on several issues (such as civil rights and school integration); and more elders were liberal on only a few issues that involved a direct benefit to the elderly (such as government support for health care).

2. *Wisdom.* This belief is based on the assumption that greater years of experience bring greater wisdom. This stereotype also has been found by several studies to be commonly associated with old age (Thomas & Yamamoto, 1975; Tuckman & Lorge, 1953). About two-thirds of Americans think most people over 65 are "very wise from experience" (Harris, 1975). This belief appears to be a reason for the predominance of older persons among judges, senators, and U.S. presidents; as well as among boards of trustees and other governing bodies (Palmore, 1988).

FACTS: There is no scientific evidence for or against this stereotype, because no one has yet developed a valid and reliable measure of wisdom (Clayton, 1987). Many assume that years of experience tend to increase wisdom, but this is an untested assumption. It is just as reasonable to assume that older age *decreases* wisdom because of the obsolescence of knowledge, withdrawal from the mainstream of life, increasing resistance to change, and so on.

3. *Dependability.* Since elders are assumed to be kinder and wiser, they are often assumed to be more dependable. For example, a survey of business managers found that they rated older workers (over age 60) as more reliable, dependable, and trustworthy than younger workers. Most people are aware of the fact that elders are the most law-abiding of all age groups (Palmore, 1988). A survey of Australian youth found that they rated elders as more responsible than younger people (Braithwaite, 1986).

FACTS: There is evidence to support this stereotype. Elders are the most law-abiding of all age groups (Cutler, 1987). They are more dependable workers: they have lower absentee rates, lower turnover rates, lower accident rates, and greater company loyalty (Palmore, 1988). There is probably less alcoholism and drug addiction among elders (Whittington, 1987; Wood, 1987).

Of course, there are many elders who do not fit this stereotype: there are numerous criminals, undependable workers, alcoholics, and drug addicts among elders. Therefore, this stereotype (like any stereotype) is not true of many elders.

4. *Affluence.* This image is one of the new axioms about elders frequently stated in news magazines and other mass media: "The aged are well off; they have been lifted out of poverty" (Binstock, 1983). This assumption is a basis for the argument that we should reduce Social Security benefits and other services to the elderly.

FACTS: This stereotype is no more true than the stereotype that most elders are poor. Over one-fifth of elders have incomes below or near (within 125%) the federal poverty levels (U.S.Senate Special Committee on Aging, 1988). Furthermore, there are certain types of elders among whom poverty is much more frequent. While 12 percent of all over 65 were below the poverty level in 1986, this figure rises to 21 percent for widowed women, to 31 percent for Blacks, and to 64 percent for Black women living alone and aged 72 or over.

Few elders would be considered "rich" by most standards: only 4 percent of families with heads aged 65 or older had incomes of $75,000 or more; and 8 percent had a net worth of $250,000 or more (U.S. Senate Special Committee on Aging, 1988).

5. *Political Power.* This stereotype is another of the new axioms about elders used to "scapegoat" the elderly: "The aged are a potent, self-interested political force" (Binstock, 1983). The assumption is that the political power of elders hamstrings our politicians from undertaking needed reforms. For example, *Newsweek* (1982) has characterized Social Security as "the third rail" of American politics and reported that the word in Congress is, "Touch it and you're dead."

FACTS: The aged do constitute a large portion of participating voters: about 16% of those who vote in national elections (Binstock, 1983). And aging-based interest groups can exert some influence, but they have not been able to swing the votes of many elders. For example, in the 1980 presidential campaign the leaders of most aging-based organizations endorsed Jimmy Carter. However, voters age 60 and over voted for him in the same proportion (54%) as did those under age 60 (*New York Times*, 1980). Thus, elders do not usually vote as a block and they therefore weaken their potential political power.

Furthermore, politicians do not usually behave as though they were strongly influenced by "senior power" (Binstock, 1983). When politicians do pass legislation favoring the elderly, they usually appear to be responding to the combined pressures exerted by elders and their many allies, such as their children and the "aging enterprise" (Estes, 1979) (see also Chapter 9).

6. *Freedom*. This belief assumes that because elders are affluent and retired, they are free to do anything they want, any time they want, any way they want. This has been called the "roleless role" of being old, or the "normless elderly" (Offenbacher & Poster, 1985). For instance, Rosow (1974) states that norms provide almost no expectations structuring an older person's activities and general patterns of life.

FACTS: It is true that most elders are free from the need to earn a living or raise children. However, they are *not* free to do "anything they want, any time they want, any way they want." There continue to be many constraints on their behavior. First, all the laws regulating behavior of other persons continue to apply to elders. Second, and perhaps even more important, most of the informal norms and expectations about proper behavior (dress, language, etiquette, duty, ethics, etc.) continue to apply to elders. There may be some relaxation of some norms (for example, elders may dress more casually than when they went to the office), but these changes are minor relative to the thousands of informal norms that continue to control behavior of elders in our culture.

Even retired elders do not have a "roleless role." They simply trade the role expectations of an employed person for the role expectations of a retired person (they should manage their financial affairs so as to remain solvent and have some assets to pass on to the next generation; they should take care of their health so as to avoid disability as long as possible; they should remain as independent as possible; they should engage in hobbies, crafts, or volunteer for useful roles to take the place of their previous work activity; etc.).

Similarly, parents whose children have grown up simply trade the role expectations of parenting for the role expectations of a grandparent (they should be willing to baby-sit and care for the grandchildren as needed; they should give the grandchildren much attention and affection; they should pass on family traditions by telling the grandchildren stories about the family and "what it was like in the old days"; etc.). They also continue to have some of the parent's role expectations (they should be available for financial and other aid when needed; they should be willing to give advice and share their knowledge and experience; they should encourage solidarity in the extended family; etc.).

7. *Eternal Youth.* Some believe that if one uses enough skin cream, wrinkle remover, hair dye, cosmetic surgery, vitamins, and exercise gadgets, one can halt aging processes. This belief is fostered by the many commercials and advertisements hawking products "guaranteed" to stop aging, or even to restore youth. As a result, Americans spend billions of dollars each years on such products.

FACTS: It is *not* possible to halt aging processes completely, although it is possible to slow or delay much of the deterioration that often occurs in old age because of inactivity, overindulgence, smoking, exposure to the sun, obesity, and so on. Longevity can be increased by healthy living and maintenance of physical and mental activity; but there is no known chemical or nutrient or activity that can prolong life beyond 125 years. At least, there is no documented case of anyone living more than 125 years.

8. *Happiness.* Finally, it is often assumed that because elders are wise, affluent, powerful, and free they must be happy. Butler (1975) calls this "the myth of serenity":

> The myth of serenity portrays old age as a kind of adult fairyland. Now at last comes a time of relative peace and serenity when people can relax and enjoy the fruits of their labors after the storms of active life are over. Advertising slogans, television and romantic fiction foster the myth. (p. 10)

FACTS: There is some evidence that somewhat more elders report more life satisfaction than younger persons, and there is somewhat less depression among elders (see stereotype of Depression above); but most elders report about the same amounts of life satisfaction, happiness, and unhappiness as when they were younger. Decreased worry about their jobs tends to be replaced by increased worry about their health and/or financial security. Decreased worry about their children tends to be replaced by increased worry about their grandchildren and children-in-laws.

POSITIVE ATTITUDES

In the section on negative attitudes we concluded that most people have mixtures of negative and some positive attitudes toward elders; and that few have predominantly positive attitudes toward the aged.

The typical positive attitude in the United States is illustrated by the popular saying (attributed to many famous older people) "Old age is not so bad compared to the alternative." But since the alternative is death, this saying really means that old age is good only in comparison to being dead. Such an attitude is barely positive. It certainly does not recognize the various advantages to old age that can be enjoyed (see Chapter 12).

Some people do look forward to their retirement thinking that it will be their "golden years." Many of these people do in fact enjoy their retirement more than their working years, often because their work has been stressful or unrewarding. However, a majority find that their happiness during the retirement years is similar to that of the working years, with a similar mix of satisfactions, problems, and frustrations. As noted above about half say "I am just as happy as when I was younger." (See also the facts on the stereotype, "Happiness," above.)

More traditional societies, such as Japan, tend to have more positive attitudes toward old age. It is polite to inquire about an older person's age in Japan, and old age is a source of pride and congratulations (Palmore, 1985). In contrast, it is rude to inquire about an older person's age in the United States because it is assumed to be a source of shame and denial. This is shown by the standard compliment given to the older person when one finds out their age: "You don't look that old." This "compliment" really means, "You don't look as decrepit and senile as most people your age."

There is also a kind of pseudopositive attitude toward old age that shows itself in various patronizing responses to elders. For example, when a "rhythm band" from a senior center or nursing home performs, we often applaud loudly and make complimentary remarks, even though the music is actually poor. This sounds positive, but actually reveals our low expectation about the musical ability of elders. It is like the saying, "It's not how well the dancing bear dances, it's that he dances at all."

Another example of this pseudopositive attitude are the complimentary remarks about the "beauty" of old people. Willard

Scott, a weatherman on a morning television show, regularly shows photographs of centenarians and comments, "Isn't she pretty?" or "Lovely lady." At best, this is a polite lie. These people are *not* beautiful by the usual standards for younger people. They can only be considered beautiful if one uses completely different standards for elders; and these standards reveal our low opinion of the appearance of elders (Cohen, 1989).

POSITIVE DISCRIMINATION

Discrimination in favor of elders can result from positive or negative stereotypes. For example, if one believed the positive stereotype that older persons are wiser, one might vote for an older candidate for judge rather than a younger one. On the other hand, if one believed the negative stereotype that the majority of aged are in poverty, one might favor special income supports for the elderly.

There is discrimination in favor of elders in five areas: economic, political, family, housing, and health care. (For discussions of whether such discrimination is desirable or not, see Part III.)

1. *Economic.* There are three major kinds of positive discrimination in the economic area practiced in our nation: tax benefits, discounts, and employment (see Chapter 8).

As for tax benefits, most state governments give a double personal exemption to all persons over 65 regardless of how rich they are. The federal government also did this until 1987, when the tax law was changed so that only the elderly who use the standard deduction (rather than itemizing deductions) get an extra deduction ($1,200 for a married couple) for being over 65. This has the effect of reducing the number of affluent aged who take advantage of this extra tax deduction.

The federal government also does not tax Social Security benefits unless the beneficiary's total income (minus one-half their Social Security benefit) is over a certain amount ($25,000 for a couple, $22,000 for a single person). Even if their income is over this amount they still pay taxes on only one-half of their Social Security.

Property tax reductions for the elderly are now granted in all states (Schulz, 1980). The most common type of reduction is a "circuit breaker." Tax relief under this mechanism is tied to need, by relating the taxpayer's income to their property tax liabilities. The amount of tax relief declines as taxpayer income rises. Another common tax benefit for the elderly is the "homestead exemption," which excludes a portion of the assessed value of a home from the taxed value.

Discounts or even free goods and services are commonly provided the elderly by drug stores, motels, restaurants, theaters, and other merchants, as well as public transportation systems and educational institutions. Presumably the rationale for these discounts is the stereotype that the elderly tend to be poor or on a fixed income. Or it may be a way to attract more business.

Although most discrimination in employment is discrimination *against* older workers, there is occasional discrimination in favor of older workers based on the stereotypes that the older worker is more dependable, wise, kind, experienced, and so on. This discrimination can occur in hiring, promotion, retention, and so on.

Such discrimination in favor of all older workers should be distinguished from seniority policies that give workers with more seniority in the company or agency certain advantages. The latter advantages are based on years of service to one employer, which may be quite different from age.

2. *Political.* Political discrimination in favor of elders takes two main forms: discrimination in favor of elders by legislators, administrators, and judges; and discrimination by voters in favor of older candidates for office (see Chapter 9). There are numerous pieces of legislation (such as Medicare) that discriminate in favor of elders. Administrators of agencies may develop policies and programs that discriminate in favor of elders based on stereotypes that they are more needy, and so on. Judges and police may discriminate in favor of older suspects or criminals based on the stereotype that most older people are basically honest and kind, or on the assumption that they do not have much longer to live and so imprisonment would be unduly harsh.

Voters often discriminate in favor of older candidates, apparently based on the stereotype that they are wiser and more judicious. Older persons are overrepresented among most elected officials and especially among the most prestigious ones such as the President, senators, and judges (Hudson & Strate, 1985).

3. *Family.* In most traditional societies the powerful heads of families tend to be elders. This is less true in the United States, but there are some examples of patriarchs and matriarchs who appear

to wield unusual power or enjoy high status partly based on their advanced age.

There are also some cases of exploitation of younger family members by the elderly, although this has not been systematically studied (see Chapter 10). There are frequent reports of daughters who are persuaded (or coerced) to sacrifice their careers and marital happiness in order to stay home and care for an elderly parent.

4. *Housing.* There are two main forms of discrimination in favor of elders in housing: government programs and private retirement communities (see Chapter 11). There are several government programs that provide low rent housing only for elders. Some of these provide public housing for elders only and some of these provide rent subsidies to private developers of housing projects for elders. There are no equivalent programs restricted to younger persons.

Many retirement communities restrict or attempt to restrict their residents to older persons. Some achieve this by prohibiting families with children in the neighborhood. Recent (1988) legislation outlaws such restrictions against children, in recognition that it is age discrimination.

5. *Health Care.* While many health professionals prefer younger patients, Medicare is a huge national health insurance program ($58 billion in 1984) that benefits only elders and the disabled (see Chapter 11). It should be remembered that rich aged as well as other aged benefit from Medicare. For younger people, the government provides health care only to the poor through Medicaid.

PERSONAL AND INSTITUTIONAL AGEISM

Personal ageism is prejudice or discrimination by individuals, while *institutional* ageism is a policy of an institution or a social structure that discriminates for or against elders, such as a compulsory retirement policy. The individuals carrying out that policy may be personally free of ageism, but they carry out the discrimination because it is part of the institution's rules (Figure 2.1).

This distinction is similar to the familiar distinction between personal racism and institutional racism (Levin & Levin, 1982). Gerontophobia and gerontophilia (next section) are examples of personal ageism, while gerontocracy is an example of institutional ageism.

GERONTOPHOBIA, GERONTOPHILIA, AND GERONTOCRACY

Gerontophobia has been defined as "unreasonable fear and/or irrational hatred of older people" (Bunzel, 1972). Bunzel claimed that it "engulfs one-fifth of the population of the United States." However, he presented no evidence for this claim. I believe that gerontophobia, in the sense of a neurosis, is only an extreme form of ageism and is actually rare in our society (Palmore, 1972b). The evidence from the many studies in this area indicates that most people have milder forms of prejudice against elders mixed with some positive stereotypes. The average American does not fear attack or serious danger from elders, nor hate elders in the dictionary sense of "to feel extreme enmity or active hostility."

On the other hand, most Americans do tend to fear their own aging. But this is primarily a fear of growing disabilities, senility, and approaching death, rather than chronological aging as such. Such fears can be reduced by learning the facts about how most aged remain relatively healthy and able until shortly before death.

Such fears may be partly unreasonable and somewhat exaggerated, but they are based on the facts of increasing rates of disability and mortality in old age. Furthermore, they do not usually interfere with normal functioning, which is the usual criteria for a neurosis. Thus, it does not seem useful to label such mild and partly rational fears as "gerontophobia." Gerontophobia should be reserved for the extreme and neurotic forms of such fear that interfere with normal functioning. Ageism is the more comprehensive term that includes all forms of prejudice and discrimination for or against elders, as well as gerontophobia.

Gerontophilia is the opposite of gerontophobia and means the love of aging and elders. It is rarely used, probably because it is even rarer than gerontophobia in our culture. Gerontophilia is more frequent in the traditional societies, especially those with a gerontocracy. It represents an extreme form of positive ageism.

Gerontocracy refers to rule by elders, or dominance by older age groups (Eisele, 1987). In popular usage, the label "gerontocratic" is usually pejorative, implying a causal connection between old age and conservative or unchanging leadership. However, such a relationship is difficult to test, but when it has been tested, the relationship has been found to be weak or nonexistent. To assume such a connection without evidence is another form of ageism.

A more scientific usage of gerontocracy refers to a society in which leadership is reserved for elders, historically almost always men. For example, the Greek city state of Sparta was ruled by a *geroursia*, or council, whose members had to be 60 and served for life. There are a number of tribes in East Africa that are geronto-cracies (Gulliver, 1968). A gerontocracy is an extreme example of discrimination in favor of elders in the political realm.

SUMMARY

Ageism may be negative (against elders) or positive (for the aged). Ageism includes both prejudice (beliefs and attitudes) and dis-crimination (actions). Thus, there are four basic types of ageism: negative prejudice, negative discrimination, positive prejudice, and positive discrimination (see Figure 2.1).

Negative prejudice in turn can be divided into negative stereo-types (beliefs) and negative attitudes (feelings). There are at least nine common stereotypes that reflect negative prejudice: the be-liefs that most aged are sick, impotent, ugly, senile, mentally ill, useless, isolated, poor, and depressed. These stereotypes are all contradicted by the facts. However, the majority of Americans have generally negative attitudes toward elders and aging. They think the older years are the worst years of a person's life. Even children tend to have negative attitudes: few prefer to be with the older man depicted in a series of drawings.

There are five major types of discrimination against elders that are common: discrimination in employment, by government agen-cies, in families, in housing, and in health care.

There are seven major positive stereotypes about elders: the beliefs that most aged are kind, wise, dependable, affluent, politi-cally powerful, free, and happy. The facts tend to contradict most of these, but there is some evidence that elders tend to be more dependable and free. There is discrimination in favor of elders in five areas: economic, political, family, housing, and health care.

Personal ageism is prejudice and discrimination by individuals, while institutional ageism is discrimination by institutions or other social structures.

Gerontophobia is an unreasonable fear or irrational hatred of older people. This phobia is rare. Gerontophilia is the love of aging and elders. This is even rarer than gerontophobia. Gerontocracy is rule by elders or dominance by older age groups.

The next chapter deals with the many different usages of terms related to ageism. Many of these usages reflect and perpetuate ageism.

3

The Meaning of Age

Second childishness and mere oblivion: sans teeth, sans eyes, sans taste, sans everything.

Shakespeare, *As You Like It*

What counts is not the age of a tire, but how much tread is left.

Senator Lloyd Bentson, 1988

POPULAR CONCEPTIONS

What does "old age" mean to the average person? When does it begin? Who identifies themselves as "old"? What are the connotations of "old"?

Do people agree that there is a chronological age at which a person becomes old? About half do, but they do not agree on what that age is. About one tenth of Americans say the average person becomes old between 50 and 59; another tenth say between 60 and 64; another tenth say between 65 and 69; and another tenth say between 70 and 79 (Harris, 1975). The other half believe that old age depends on factors such as retirement status, senility, and so on. Furthermore, there is no more agreement among elders than among the young as to when one becomes "old." Thus, there is little consensus about the beginning of old age. This may be because the negative connotations of old age make people want to deny its onset.

Those who believe most people over 65 are "very useful" tend to think that people become old after they are 65, while those who believe that old people are "not useful" tend to accept the idea that a person is old at 65 (Harris, 1975). Thus, people seem to equate being old with being useless.

One might think that people over 75 would certainly define themselves as old or elderly. The majority do, but about a quarter still maintain that they are "young" or "middle-aged" (Palmore, 1970). It is clear that many deny their old age, even at advanced ages. This is probably based on a denial of the negative connotations of "old age" (see Chapter 7).

Perhaps the most famous popular conception of old age was provided by Shakespeare in *As You Like It:* "Sans teeth, sans eyes, sans taste, sans everything." This is one of the most negative conceptions in popular culture, and yet it is often accepted as defining the last stage of life. It is understandable why people would want to deny that they belong to such a miserable group.

The basic problem here is the confusion between "old" in the sense of chronological age and "old" in the sense of worn out, useless, outmoded, obsolete, or discarded (Webster's Dictionary, 1984). Logically, chronologically "old" need not have these negative connotations. But in popular usage "old" is used to refer to both the chronologically aged *and* to people who are worn out, useless, or debilitated (see Chapter 6). This is what is meant by the phrase "feeling old." To "look old" usually means to look ugly and/or decrepit. To say "You don't look that old" is a compliment meaning "You don't look as senile and decrepit as most people your age look." "To age rapidly" means to deteriorate rapidly.

Similarly, "young" has the connotations of vigorous, active, and healthy. This is what is meant by the phrases "young at heart" and "feeling young again." To "look young" usually means to look more vigorous, beautiful, or handsome. Obviously such connotations of "old" and "young" tend to create and reinforce ageism. (See section on "Language" in Chapter 6.)

AGING VS. DYING

A similar source of ageism is the confusion between aging and dying. As Melvin Konner (1988, p. 100) has recently observed, "(In America) the fear of death and the fear of aging are one. Only the old die; therefore if one avoids growing old, one will surely avoid dying."

Normal aging processes need not be negative; they need not cause declines in health or functioning abilities. On the contrary, there are often positive aspects to aging such as decreased allergic reactions, fewer acute illnesses, fewer accidents, less substance abuse, less crime victimization, more economic security, more maturity and wisdom, freedom from child rearing and the necessity to work, and so on. (Palmore, 1979; see also "Advantages of Aging" in Chapter 12). Thus, old age *can be* the "golden years" and the consummation of life that many people enjoy more than any other age.

On the other hand, the dying process, regardless of the age at which it occurs, is usually negative; it involves degeneration, disability, dependence, pain, and misery. The problem arises when people confuse these two different processes and assume that aging processes are also negative because aging is "just a prelude to death." They see or read about the miserable terminal cases in nursing homes and think of them as typical of old people rather than of dying people. They fail to realize that most old people are not dying, but are able to carry out their normal activities (Palmore, 1988).

If people could distinguish between aging and dying; if they could realize that death can happen at any age and does not necessarily have anything to do with aging, they would have less negative attitudes toward aging. To put it in an aphorism, "Dying is the enemy, not aging." (Of course, dying may not be an enemy to those suffering from unbearable physical or mental pain.)

LEGAL DEFINITIONS

Because the government restricts certain programs and benefits to elders, the government must use unambiguous chronological definitions of who is aged. In fact the government uses a wide range of definitions depending on the program or benefit. The U.S. Department of Labor defines an "older worker" as being age 40 or over! At age 50 one may participate in "Senior Games" sponsored by state agencies on aging and departments of recreation. At age 60 one may participate in most senior centers, and widows become eligible for survivor benefits under Social Security. At age 62 people become eligible to live in housing for the elderly and draw reduced retirement benefits under Social Security. At age 65 one may draw the normal Social Security retirement benefit and become eligible for Medicare. At age 72, the Social Security Administration drops its reduction of benefits for earnings.

Thus, there is no legal consensus on when old age arrives, just as there is no popular consensus. This is probably based on the fact that there is no one chronological age, nor range of ages, in which most people change from the characteristics of middle-aged to those of old age. On the contrary, most people change slowly as they age, and the rates of change vary greatly between individuals. Therefore, any chronological definition of old age must be arbitrary and of limited usefulness.

FUNCTIONAL DEFINITIONS

There have been some attempts to define "functional age," based on the fact that chronological age has little relationship to functional ability and therefore is not a useful indicator of ability to work or to remain independent. Functional age was first used by McFarland (1973) to suggest that the individual's capacity, rather than chronological age, be used as the marker for ability in the workplace.

However, as Siegler (1988) pointed out, the concept of functional age has little practical utility for research. There are several problems with the concept. First, there are many different dimensions involved in functional ability. There is physical ability, mental ability, social ability, economic ability, political ability, and so on. In fact, there are hundreds of different kinds of abilities. Each of these abilities may vary independently of the others. Therefore, there is no way to usefully summarize an individual's many abilities along a single dimension.

It may be possible to specify the major abilities needed for a particular job, to measure an individual's skill in these abilities, and to somehow summarize these skills into a single rating. But the resulting "functional age" would be meaningful only for that job and not for jobs requiring different abilities.

Furthermore, such a "functional age" would have little relationship to chronological age, so why use the term "age" at all? It would be better to call it "functional ability" for a specified job. The entire attempt to relate age and ability seems fruitless, and serves only to increase the confusion between two independent dimensions. This confusion supports ageism because it assumes that "older" means more disabled.

BIOLOGICAL DEFINITIONS

A group of biological gerontologists have defined aging as "any time-dependent change, common to all members of a species, which occurs after maturity of size, form, or function is reached and which is distinct from daily, seasonal, and other biological rhythms" (Rockstein & Sussman, 1979). This theoretically includes all the postmaturational physical changes in an individual: both declines (senescence) and improvements (such as fewer acute illnesses and reduced allergic reactions).

However, in practice biological gerontologists have focused on senescence and have neglected the study of factors related to improvements or maintenance of function. This emphasis on senescence tends to support the ageist assumption that aging is nothing but declines and deteriorations.

This focus on senescence also encourages the attitude of "victim-blaming" (Levin & Levin, 1980). Victim-blaming is the tendency to blame a social problem (in this case ageism) on the characteristics of the people who are its victims. Thus, the prejudices and discriminations against elders are justified by the supposed characteristics of the aged themselves (see Chapter 6). Older workers are forced to retire because they are "obsolete" and no longer "competent." Older people are denied some government services because they are "too old to benefit" from the program. Families ignore or abuse older members because they are "senile."

It is a biological fact that mortality rates increase with age during adulthood. Therefore, the average number of years remaining before death decrease as chronological age increases. This is true on a group (actuarial) basis but is not very useful on an individual basis, because the individual years remaining before death vary greatly within any given age group. Some will die within a year and some will live for many more years.

Furthermore, it can be argued that people at a given age, say 65, are now biologically much "younger" than people age 65 in previous generations. Certainly the actuarial remaining life expectancy of today's 65-year-old has increased substantially in the last 25 or 50 years. There is also evidence that the amount of disability among those over 65 has declined since 1965 (Palmore, 1986; Crimmins et al., 1989).

But once again, to say that today's 65-year-olds are now "younger" than previous 65-year-olds is to confuse chronological age with functional ability or health or longevity. Such confusion could be reduced if we did not use "young" and "old" to mean able or disabled, healthy or sick.

PSYCHOLOGICAL VIEWS

Child psychologists have created useful *stage theories* in which successive stages of childhood are qualitatively different, but most students of adult development and aging have not found stage theories useful (Neugarten, 1977). This is because a true stage theory has qualitatively different stages that form a cluster of behaviors that cross-cut various types of behavior, and that form an invariant and irreversible order (Kohlberg, 1973). Such criteria do not fit the reality of adulthood and aging, where there are few qualitative changes, where there is no clear biological timetable, and where major life events (widowhood, retirement, menopause) occur in various orders.

However, there are more generally used markers of *life periods*. In all societies the differences between infants, adults, and elders have been recognized, and typical characteristics have been ascribed to each period. In modern society life periods have been increasingly differentiated so that we now recognize childhood, adolescence, young adulthood, and middle age in addition to the universal periods listed above.

It has been found that perceptions of such life periods tend to vary by age, sex, and by social class. For example, upper-middle-class people tend to describe middle age as a period of greater productivity and of major reward, the "prime of life," while blue-collar workers usually describe it in terms of decline—slowing down, weakening, becoming a "has-been" (Hagestad & Neugarten, 1985).

However, few personality psychologists have used these periods in studying adult personality change (Erikson, 1968; Kastenbaum, 1987a). Thus, there is little developed theory and even less good research on personality differences between elders and younger persons. The research that exists shows much greater variability in personality *within* these age categories than between them. Thus any attempt to distinguish general personality differences between elders and others is premature at best, and may be hopeless. At present, such attempts tend to result in ageist stereotypes.

SOCIOLOGICAL VIEWS

Although sociological theory is intended to be value free and unbiased, some sociological perspectives on aging may have ageist implications or may be used to reinforce ageism. One such perspective is the "social problems" approach to old age. This approach recognizes that many aged suffer from poverty, isolation, poor health, uselessness, and so on and asks what are the causes of this situation and how might it be changed.

The difficulty with this approach comes when it is assumed that elders themselves cause the problem because there are too many of them, they are too feeble to be useful, they are obsolete, they are too sick and demand too much medical care, and so on. This is the same pattern of victim blaming discussed above.

The problems elders suffer in our society are usually called "the problems of aging." But to the extent that these problems are the result of ageism by the young, the problems are misnamed. According to Rosow (1962), the problems are really problems of the young: "The crucial people in the aging problems are not the old, but the younger age groups, for it is the rest of us who determine the status and position of the old person in the social order" (p. 191). Thus, it might better be renamed "the problems of the non-aged."

Furthermore, the entire preoccupation with "the problems of the aged" ignores the "opportunities of elders." The problem approach neglects the positive side of aging: the advantages, the skills, the wisdom, the growth potential, and the contributions elders can make.

Similarly, some theories in social gerontology, such as disengagement and subculture theory, have been interpreted in ways that support ageism. Disengagement theory asserts that it is natural, normal, and desirable for elders to disengage (Cumming & Henry, 1961). This tends to perpetuate the stereotypes of elders as useless, withdrawn, inactive, and isolated. Most research has shown that while there tends to be some disengagement with aging, most elders maintain many of their preretirement activities and find new activities and relationships to replace the old (Palmore, 1981).

Subculture theory asserts that elders have a distinctive subculture based on common physiological, economic, and status-loss problems (Longino, 1987). Because of ageism in our culture, most elders do not want to be identified as aged and therefore often insulate themselves from status-loss by segregating themselves from others. At the same time, their age-based solidarity may foster a social movement aimed at changing the cultural definition of aging from negative to positive. A number of studies of age-concentrated housing has provided limited support for this theory (Longino, McClelland, & Peterson, 1980).

To the extent that subculture theory exaggerates the extent of withdrawal from contact with younger persons, and exaggerates the distinctiveness of elders' subculture, it supports the stereotypes of withdrawn, old-fashioned, and abnormal aged. To the extent that it recognizes the potential for a social movement against ageism, it may encourage the reduction of ageism.

On the other hand, some social gerontology theories have tended to oppose ageism. Age stratification theory (Riley, 1987) has emphasized such processes as age segregation, age strata conflict, and age norms, all of which tend to blame the system rather than the individual aged for their problems. Also, activity and reengagement theory (Jacobs & Vinick, 1977) have suggested the efficacy of not treating elders as a special group distinguishable from the middle aged.

Minority group theory (as in Levin & Levin, 1980) has made a major contribution to the recognition of ageism as a source of the problems of older people in our society. Many of the insights of this book are drawn from parallels in the literature on racism and sexism.

Many social gerontologists have also emphasized the diversity of elders. They have emphasized that there are as many different types of older people as there are younger people: healthy and sick, rich and poor, happy and sad, smart and dumb, good and bad. Recently many have emphasized the great differences between the "young-old" (age 65–74), the "middle-old" (age 75–84), and the "old-old" (age 85 and over) (Neugarten, 1974; Atchley, 1987a).

Maddox and Douglas (1985) found that heterogeneity tends to be maintained or to increase among elders over time. In other words, elders tend to become more different from each other as they age, rather than more alike. Thus, it is not accurate or useful to assume that most elders are basically alike, that "once you've seen one, you've seen them all." This assumption is usually accompanied by a negative view of elders. The research and writing that emphasizes the diversity among elders tends to counteract such ageist assumptions.

Some social gerontologists write about different "life stages" among the elderly. For example, the most popular text in the field (Atchley, 1988) distinguishes between "middle age" (which usually begins around age 40), "later maturity" (usually begins in the sixties), and "old age" (typically occurs in the late seventies). Atchley asserts that these stages are not based on chronological age, but on sets of related characteristics. For example,

> Old age is characterized by extreme physical frailty. . . . Mental processes slow down; organic brain disease becomes more common. The individual in old age feels that death is near. Activity is greatly restricted. Social networks have been decimated. . . . Institutionalization is common. This stage of life is apt to be unpleasant. (pp. 7–8)

A popularized version of the young-old, middle-old, and old-old stages calls them the "go-go," the "slow-go," and the "no-go." The "go-go" aged are defined as the younger, more active persons (usually in their sixties); the "slow-go" are those who are slowing down and disengaging (usually in their seventies); and the "no-go" are those who are feeble and frail (usually 80 and over).

As appealing as such conceptions may appear to be on a common sense level, there are two problems with such stage concepts. First, they are inevitably associated with certain chronological ages (such as over 85 for the "old-old"). As a result, we end up with a new set of stereotypes associated with certain chronological ages. To be sure, the new stereotypes are differentiated by smaller age ranges, but they remain stereotypes nevertheless. As such, they do not fit the majority of the individuals in the age range. For example, the majority of persons over 85 are not in poor health, do not have organic brain disease, do not have decimated social networks, are not institutionalized, and do not report that life is unpleasant (Rosenwaike, 1985).

Secondly, these stereotypes tend to emphasize the negative aspects of aging and especially of the older stages (as can be seen from the above quotation from Atchley). They ignore the satisfactions of achieving advanced longevity, and the wisdom, skills, respect, and serenity that often accompany it.

SUMMARY

There is no consensus about when old age begins or even whether it begins at a fixed chronological age. Even among those over 75, a quarter still maintain that they are not old. This denial of old age is caused by the negative connotations of "old" such as worn out, useless, obsolete, ugly, and senile. Similarly, "young" has positive connotations such as vigorous, beautiful, fresh, and capable. Another negative connotation of aging is its association with dying. If people would distinguish between aging and dying, they might have less negative attitudes toward aging.

The U.S. government definitions of when old age begins range from age 40 (for older workers) to age 72 (when Social Security drops its reduction of benefits for earnings). This lack of consensus is related to the fact that there is no fixed chronological age, nor range of ages, in which most people show some qualitative change. On the contrary, most people change gradually, if at all, and at extremely different rates. Therefore, any chronological definition of old age must be arbitrary and of limited usefulness.

Biological definitions of aging theoretically include all post-maturational physical changes: both declines and improvements. In practice, however, they tend to focus on the declines and neglect the maintenance or improvement of function. This tends to encourage the attitude of victim-blaming, in which the victims of ageism are blamed for the discrimination against them.

Most psychologists studying adult personality have not found stage theories useful. Our society generally recognizes distinctions between infants, children, adolescents, young adults, middle-aged, and elders. However, the personality research that has been done shows more variability within the elders category than between it and younger adult categories. Attempts to characterize "elders' personality" are premature at best, and tend to result in ageist stereotypes.

Some sociological views of aging tend to support ageism. For example, the social problems approach often assumes that the problem is caused primarily by characteristics of elders. The concern with the "problems of aging" ignores the opportunities and advantages of aging. Similarly, disengagement and subculture theory have been interpreted in ways that support ageism.

Other sociological views tend to reduce ageism. For example, age stratification theory tends to blame the system rather than elders for their problems. Reengagement theory tends to treat elders as any other age group. Minority group theory recognizes ageism as a major source of the problems of older people in our society. The emphasis on diversity among elders tends to break down stereotypes.

This completes our discussion of basic concepts in ageism. The next part analyzes the various causes and consequences of ageism, starting with the individual causes.

Part II
Causes and
Consequences

4

Individual Sources

Certain types of personality are prejudice-prone; a wide variety of needs may be served by prejudice.

Simpson & Yinger, 1985

THE AUTHORITARIAN PERSONALITY

The above quotation comes from a popular text, *Racial and Cultural Minorities*, but it probably applies to prejudice against elders as well. A great deal of research has tended to support the theory that prejudice is often part of a complicated personality syndrome called "the authoritarian personality" (Adorno, Frenel-Brunswick, Levinson, & Sanford, 1950). According to this theory, prejudice is often a manifestation of basic insecurity, of repressed impulses, of a belief that life is capricious and threatening, and an emphasis upon competitive power in human relationships. Other characteristics of such personalities are rigidity of outlook, intolerance of ambiguity, pseudoscientific or antiscientific attitudes, suggestibility and gullibility, and unrealistic views about what will achieve goals.

Various studies have found that authoritarian personalities tend to be less intelligent and less educated (Christie & Cook, 1958), tend to dislike or distrust people in general (Sullivan & Adelson, 1954), and tend to be more rigid mentally (Rokeach, 1948).

Similarly, various studies have found that those with negative attitudes toward elders also tend to be less educated (Thorson, Whatley, & Hancock, 1974; Palmore, 1988). One study found that prejudice against elders correlated significantly with death anxiety: the more anxious were more prejudiced (Palmore, 1988). Levin & Levin (1980) theorize

> certain individuals—those who are excessively concerned with their status and the maintenance of their self-esteem—express a generalized hostility directed against the members of any group regarded as weak, powerless, or inferior. Based on their stereotyped public image as declining, sexless, and disengaged, and their vulnerable position in our society, we might suspect that aged Americans would be disliked by the same individuals who hate members of other minorities, and for the same reasons. (pp. 91f)

Kogan (1973) directly tested this hypothesis among 482 undergraduate students and found it to be true: "There is a general trend for subjects to be positive or negatively disposed toward a wide variety of groups deviating in some respect from a hypothetical norm of similarity to self" (p.53).

He also found that the more prejudiced subjects were also more likely to be anomic: that is, they were more pessimistic about the future, feel helpless in the face of powerful social forces, and feel incapable of finding meaning or purpose in life. It is understandable how such feelings are likely to result in negative views of aging and elders.

Although the theory linking the authoritarian personality to ageism has not been thoroughly tested, the existing evidence suggests that the same personality traits that contribute to racism may also contribute to ageism. Further research is needed to test the validity of this hypothesis.

FRUSTRATION-AGGRESSION THEORY

There is much evidence to indicate that frustrating events often cause hostile impulses in the individual (Simpson & Yinger, 1985). In many instances this hostility cannot be directed toward the real source of the frustration; there may be no human agent, or the agent may be unknown, or the agent may be too powerful to attack, or the frustration may result from inner conflict.

In such situations the hostility may be displaced against some innocent minority-group members who are vulnerable to attack. The minority-group members thus become scapegoats for the hostility generated by the frustration. Such an attack must be justified or rationalized somehow so that the attacker can feel reasonable and moral. Stereotypes come into play to rationalize discrimination against the whole group, despite the variations that characterize any human group.

We have seen how ageism tends to be stronger in the lower socioeconomic classes (Palmore, 1988), those who are likely to be more frustrated by poverty and low status. It may be that their greater prejudice against older persons may be caused by their greater frustration.

Binstock (1983) has described a recent example of using "elders as scapegoat." He said that in the early 1980s, elders were "bearing the blame for a variety òf economic and political frustrations" such as a depressed economy, high rates of unemployment and inflation, and the budget deficit. This scapegoating was based on three false stereotypes: that elders are well off; that they have too much political power; and that they pose an unsustainable burden on the U.S. economy. These stereotypes were being encouraged by statements from some leaders in the administration and by sensationalism in the mass media.

He concluded that this scapegoating has three deleterious effects: it diverts our attention from a variety of deficiencies in public leadership and public policy; it is engendering intergenerational conflict; and it is diverting our attention from issues of reform in government benefit policies.

SELECTIVE PERCEPTION

This is a well-known phenomenon in psychology and especially in minority group relations. It is a major explanation for the persistence of stereotypes in the face of contrary evidence. Simply stated, we tend to see what we expect to see. Hamilton (1981) observes that we often should reverse the old adage about seeing and believing to make it read: "I wouldn't have seen it if I hadn't believed it" (p. 137).

This tendency to perceive confirming evidence and to ignore disconfirming evidence is especially strong in the case of ageist stereotypes, because we do not usually know the actual chronological age of older persons. *We usually infer people's age from their characteristics*. Thus, when we see people who are gray-haired, wrinkled, stooped, or feeble, we infer that they are old; when in fact they might be younger persons who have had some illness or disability. Whereas when we see people who are dark-haired, smooth skinned, erect, and vigorous, we infer that they are not old; when in fact they may be older than the first person, but are in good health, dye their hair, and have had a face lift.

In either case, our perceptions tend to confirm our stereotype because we only identify as old those who fit our stereotype of old people. The fact that most people over 65 do not fit our stereotype *is not perceived* precisely because they do not fit our stereotype.

This is a major problem in attempts to change stereotypes. For example, most viewers probably perceive Angela Lansbury, the heroine of *Murder She Wrote*, as "middle-aged" rather than an "old woman" because she is so healthy, vigorous, and clever. In fact, she is 65 years old (in 1990) and would be eligible for Social Security benefits if she retired. For another example, few think of Mike Wallace, the famous television reporter, as an "old man" because he also is healthy, vigorous, and an excellent interviewer. In fact, he is 71 years old! For a third example, Zsa Zsa Gabor is not thought of as "old" because she is so glamorous. She is at least 71 and possibly 73, although she now claims to be only 60.

RATIONALIZATION

This is another well known psychological process supporting prejudice and discrimination. Rationalization is the process of attributing one's actions to rational and creditable motives without analysis of true (especially unconscious) motives (Webster, 1984). A classic example in race relations is the segregation of Blacks being rationalized as necessary to "keep the white race pure," rather than admitting that segregation is designed to keep Blacks subjugated.

In the area of ageism, rationalization can take many forms. Forced retirement may be rationalized on the grounds that the older worker is no longer competent, or is slowing down, or is old-fashioned, or is unattractive; when the primary reason is to replace a higher paid (older) worker with a lower paid (younger) worker.

Putting an older relative into a nursing home may be rationalized on the grounds that "it is for their own good"; when the primary reason is to avoid the burdens of caregiving at home. Confining a nursing home patient to a chair with restraints may be rationalized on the grounds that it is for the patient's own protection; rather than admitting that the primary reason is to reduce the attention demanded by the patient.

Doctors may rationalize their neglect of older patients on the grounds that their illness is "due to old age" and will not respond to treatment; when the primary reason is that they do not get as high a fee from Medicare for treating older patients as they do for treating younger patients.

The segregation and avoidance of older people may be rationalized on the grounds that "they prefer to be with their age group"; when the primary reason is that younger persons unconsciously associate old age with death and want to avoid thinking about death. Jokes about elders may be told "because they are funny"; when the primary reason is to satisfy a need to feel superior to some lower status or less capable group.

Positive discrimination for elders can also be rationalized. Special discounts for elders may be rationalized on the grounds that they are on fixed incomes and cannot afford to pay full prices; when the main motivation is advertising and marketing the product.

The provision of Medicare for elders only may be rationalized on the grounds that elders cannot afford to pay for their medical bills as well as younger people; when the main reason is the avoidance of a national health insurance system for all ages.

GERONTOPHOBIA AND DEATH ANXIETY

As indicated in Chapter 2, gerontophobia is defined as "the unreasonable fear or irrational hatred of older people" (Bunzel, 1972). It may be based on an extreme form of death anxiety in which elders are feared because they are associated with death, and death is feared more than anything.

This type of gerontophobia is stronger in modern developed societies than in earlier societies because in modern societies death rates increase sharply in old age, whereas in earlier societies death rates were more equal at younger and older ages. Therefore, one's chances of dying in a given year did not increase much with age, and so old age was not so closely associated with death.

Similarly, aging may be feared because it is assumed that each year older brings one closer to death. This is true, but it should be balanced by the equal truth that each year survived extends one's life expectancy (or expected age at death) by several months. For example, each year survived beyond 65 increases life expectancy by about five months (National Center for Health Statistics, 1986).

Gerontophobia may be caused by some traumatic experience in childhood (or later) with some aged person who abused the child or otherwise caused great fear. Even if such an experience is repressed, it can continue to cause gerontophobia. Such extreme phobias usually need professional therapy to be reduced.

SUMMARY

Authoritarian personalities tend to be prejudiced against a variety of racial and ethnic groups. There is evidence that they are also prejudiced against elders. Similarly, frustration has been shown to be a cause of prejudice against minority groups, through a process in which the minority group is blamed and becomes a scapegoat for the frustration. The aged may also become scapegoats for frustrations experienced in our society.

The tendency for selective perception, in which people perceive what they expect to perceive, is a major explanation for the persistence of stereotypes. This is especially important in ageist stereotypes because we do not usually perceive people as aged unless they fit our stereotype of an old person.

Rationalization is another psychological process that supports prejudice and discrimination. It attributes one's actions to creditable motives without analysis of the true motives. Both positive and negative discrimination against elders are often rationalized on the basis of stereotypes about elders.

Gerontophobia may be based on death anxiety because people in our society tend to associate old age with death. Gerontophobia may also be caused by suffering from abuse in childhood by an aged person.

These individual psychological processes show that prejudice in general and ageism in particular can be partially explained by an individual's personality, modes of perception and thinking, and childhood experiences. We now turn to a discussion of how social and cultural forces channel an individual's tendency toward prejudice into negative or positive ageism.

5

Social Influences

If men define situations as real, they will be real in their consequences.
W. I. Thomas

The traditional tradeoff between guns and butter may in the future be better characterized as a tradeoff between guns and canes.
Torrey, 1982

MODERNIZATION THEORY

The basic idea of modernization and aging theory is that the changes from preindustrial to industrial societies cause declines in the status and prestige of elders (Cowgill, 1974). This devaluation is caused by several factors associated with modernization:

1. Lowered birth and death rates produce a higher proportion of aged in the population. This makes the supply of older persons exceed the demand.
2. The increased use of technology and automation decreases the demand for older workers.
3. Rapidly changing technology and new occupations make the job skills of older workers obsolete.
4. Increased retirement lowers the income and social status of elders.
5. Child-centered education and rapid social change make obsolete much of the knowledge that formerly was a basis for prestige of elders.

6. Urbanization often leaves the elderly behind in rural areas or deteriorated parts of the city, further reducing their status and prestige.

There has been some controversy about whether these changes occurred before, during, or after the decline in the status of elders (Achenbaum, 1978; Fischer, 1978); but it seems clear that these processes of modernization contribute to their decline in status, whether or not the processes were the first causes.

Similarly, such processes also contribute to ageism. The "excess" of older workers competing for jobs tends to make younger workers hostile to them. The obsolescence of older persons' skills and knowledge tends to make them appear old-fashioned and useless. Retirement tends to lower power and prestige. Concentrations of elders in rural and deteriorated areas tends to support prejudice against them.

However, there is some recent evidence that suggests two modifications to the basic theory of modernization and aging. First, there are some societies, such as Japan, in which the culture (filial piety and respect for seniors) and social structure ("vertical" rather than "horizontal") tend to counteract the effects of modernization on the status and prestige of elders. While modernization in Japan has caused some decline in the status and prestige of the elderly, their social integration and respect has remained high compared to that in Western societies (Palmore, 1985). Thus, modernization theory needs to recognize that the negative effects of modernization can be at least partially ameliorated by culture and social structure.

Secondly, in the postindustrial societies, such as the United States, the status and prestige of the elderly may be increasing because of their increasing income, education, and health (Palmore, 1974, 1976, 1986). Furthermore, increasing knowledge about the facts on aging through the growth of both gerontology and media attention tends to diminish the old negative stereotypes (Palmore, 1988). Thus, modernization may have negative effects in the early stages, but have positive effects after the industrial revolution.

HISTORY OF AGEISM IN THE UNITED STATES

In Colonial times the elderly were relatively rare: about two percent of the population (U.S. Bureau of Census, 1984b). Yet those few usually enjoyed an advantaged position because old age was given higher status and respect in the major institutions of the society.

In the religious institutions, the Bible's traditional respect for elders was expanded into a moral veneration of elders. The ruling body in the local church was often called "The Board of Elders." In agriculture, control of the land gave the elders extensive power. In crafts and trade, the skill and experience of the elders gave them more success and power than younger persons. In the Revolutionary War "gray champions" like Deacon Josiah Haynes, who led the Minutemen of Sudbury at age 80, were the basis for the symbol of "Uncle Sam" with his gray beard (Fischer, 1978).

In Reisman's terminology (1950), Colonial America was a "tradition-directed" society in which older people instructed younger people in correct behavior according to traditions. Therefore the older people tended to have higher status and more prestige because of their age and superior knowledge of the traditions.

In such a society positive ageism was the rule, with prejudice and discrimination usually directed against younger people, rationalized on the basis of their supposed lack of maturity, wisdom, skill, and so on.

After the Revolutionary War, there was an accelerated emphasis on equality, individual achievement, secularism, and the free market. All these ideologies tended to undercut the advantages that elders traditionally enjoyed in Colonial times. Also the rapid increase in the population and land area of the United States encouraged much geographic mobility. This too undercut the traditional authority of older persons in the family and community.

In Riesman's terms, the postrevolution United States became an "inner-directed" society in which individuals were guided by internalized norms and values that were adaptable to changing situations, rather than by the rigid traditions of the past. Thus, parents were important for instilling these norms in children, but once their children internalized the norms, they no longer needed the detailed guidance of parents and other older persons.

The new patterns did not yet put the elderly at a disadvantage, but tended to support a more realistic balance between the advantages and liabilities of aging. In other words, there was a decrease in the positive ageism typical of Colonial times.

After the Civil War, rapid modernization and urbanization took place in the United States. The six processes listed at the begining of this chapter began to lower the status and prestige of the elders.

In addition, several other factors tended to encourage the growth of negative ageism.

As science began to replace religion and tradition as sources of knowledge, it began to document the *average* declines in physical functioning and the increases in chronic disease with aging. Cross-sectional studies found lower average mental capacities in older age groups. These studies were the basis for the ageist view of aging as inevitable decline. Only in the last two or three decades has modern gerontology developed alternative views such as compensation theory, activity theory, and continuity theory, based on longitudinal studies (see Chapter 6).

Another factor related to modernization was a greater emphasis on individual achievement and efficiency. This emphasis often worked to the disadvantage of older workers who could not keep up with younger workers in terms of speed or strength. This was especially true on the speeded-up assembly lines created by "scientific management."

Also pension plans began to spread, primarily as a way to discourage older skilled workers from changing jobs (Haber, 1987). This had the secondary effect of making retirement possible for more workers. Furthermore, mandatory retirement became widespread as a way to limit the seniority rights of older workers. As we have noted, retirement in those days tended to lower income and prestige.

A final factor contributing to the rise of negative ageism around the turn of the century was the increased competition between the older native workers and the younger immigrant workers who would work for lower wages. Employers interested in maximizing profits found that replacing older (high wage) workers with younger (low wage) workers could do wonders for their balance sheets.

This incentive to reduce labor costs, and the myth of rapid decline in old age, combined to produce widespread discrimination against elders in employment. More and more older workers were singled out for layoff, firing, or compulsory retirement. And once fired, they had extreme difficulty in finding another job because of age discrimination in hiring practices.

Some of these unemployed or retired workers were fortunate enough to have a private pension or some savings to fall back on, but many had only their family or the dreaded "poor house" or "old folks homes" to take care of them. Avoiding the "poor house" became a major security goal of Americans in the early 1900s and led to the enactment of the Social Security Act of 1935.

This situation helped to perpetuate the stereotype that the majority of the aged are poor. This stereotype was, in fact, true before the coming of Social Security, which was designed to eliminate poverty among elders. We have seen that Social Security has been successful in reducing poverty among elders to levels lower than that among the the rest of the population.

Even before the coming of Social Security, some popular books began to appear with titles like *Life Begins at Forty*, which stressed the more positive aspects of aging (Achenbaum, 1978). Also, some scientists began developing more positive views of aging, such as Dr. I. L. Nascher, who stressed the body's ability to renew itself and maintain good health in later life. Nevertheless, prejudice and discrimination against elders continued at high levels until after World War II.

During and after World War II, several developments took place that began to improve the image and status of elders. One of the most dramatic changes was the rapid increase in the number of aged. Between 1940 and 1960 the older population nearly doubled. According to modernization theory, this increase in elders population should have had the effect of lowering their status, because the "supply" of aged would exceed the "demand" for elders. This was probably true earlier in this century, but several things happened that prevented this effect during World War II.

First, because of the labor shortage during the war, industry used all the older workers it could get. Secondly, the growth of Social Security and private pensions made retirement more and more attractive. The increase in retirement more than compensated for the increase in number of older people. The net effect of the rapid increase in elders population was mainly to increase their political influence and to increase the number and scope of various public and private programs to improve the status of elders.

Another development after World War II was the steady improvement in retirement income. This improvement was brought about by three main factors: improvement in the coverage and benefit levels of Social Security; a tripling of the number of workers covered by private pensions; and the general increase in affluence that most elders shared (Atchley, 1982). This development reduced the amount of poverty, which in turn began to undercut the stereotype that most aged lived in poverty.

In the 1960s three major bills passed that also began to improve the circumstances of elders: the *Older Americans Act*, the *Medicare and Medicaid* bill, and the *Age Discrimination in Employment Act.* The *Older Americans Act* established the Administration on Aging and authorized grants for planning, coordination of services, and training. *Medicare and Medicaid* provided health insurance for elders and poor. The *Age Discrimination in Employment Act* prohibited the use of age as a criterion for hiring, firing, discriminatory treatment on the job, by employment agencies, in advertisements, and by unions. However, it did not protect workers over the age of 65!

This was rectified by the 1978 *Age Discrimination in Employment Act,* which raised to 70 the ages protected, and by the 1986 amendments, which eliminated the age cap altogether. However, the 1986 amendments did allow four exceptions to its prohibition against compulsory retirement: tenured faculty 70 years of age or over; executives entitled to at least $44,000 a year in retirement benefits; public officials and their staff not subject to civil service laws; and firefighters and law enforcement personnel. Otherwise, it is now illegal to discriminate in any way against older persons in employment. This has been a major step in reducing (but not eliminating) a major form of discrimination in our society.

In the 1970s other major legislation further improved the situation of elders. The *Older Americans Act* was amended to provide for a national network of agencies serving the elderly. *Supplemental Security Income* began to provide a minimum income for all persons over 65. The *Employees Retirement Income Security Act* (ERISA) imposed federal standards on private pension plans. The National Institute on Aging was added to the National Institutes of Health to fund and organize research on aging.

Also in the 1970s there was rapid growth in the membership of organizations for elders. The American Association of Retired Persons (AARP) grew to over 6 million members (now about 30 million members). The National Council of Senior Citizens grew to over 3 million. These large numbers were able to combat ageism in three ways: they could employ skilled lobbyists in Washington; they published magazines such as *Modern Maturity,* which emphasizes a positive view of aging; and they provided many services, such as discount drugs and travel, to improve the health and life-style of the elderly.

Other developments since World War II will be dealt with in Part III.

DEMOGRAPHICS

The most dramatic demographic change has been the rapid increase in the sheer number of elderly in the United States (see Figure 5.1). In 1890 there were only 2.4 million persons age 65 or over. This number had doubled by 1920; doubled again by 1940; doubled a third time by 1970; and is expected to double a fourth time by 2010 (U.S. Bureau of the Census, 1984b). Of course the population under age 65 was also increasing, but not at such a rapid rate. As a result, the proportion of the total population over age 65 also increased. In 1890 elders were about 4 percent of the total; this percentage did not double until 1950 (when it was 8 percent); and probably will not double again (to 16%) until 2020. At present elders constitute almost 13 percent of the total population.

This increase in the older population has had several contrary effects on ageism. As indicated above, the early increase when there was also increasing competition in the work force from

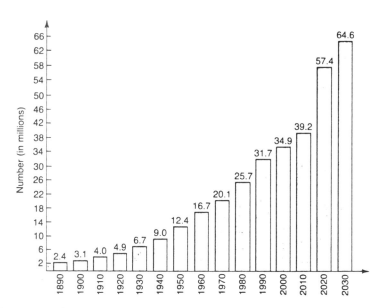

Figure 5.1 Number of person 65 or over in the United States, 1890–2030. Source: U.S. Bureau of Census, 1984b.

younger immigrant workers, tended to increase prejudice and discrimination against elders. But the later increase, when there was less competition with younger workers, resulted in extensive legislation and programs to improve the situation of elders. This has tended to gradually change the image of the elderly to a more positive one.

While the over 65 group has been increasing rapidly, the over 85 group has been increasing even more rapidly. While the total older population is expected to double between 1960 and 2000, those over 85 will nearly quintuple! This means that the group most needing health and social services is increasing most rapidly. Furthermore, the working age population (18–64) is expected to remain about the same size. This is creating acute concern about the burden on our health and social service facilities. The effect of this on ageism is unclear at present.

Another demographic trend among elders is the increasing proportion who are women. In 1960 55 percent of those over 65 were women; by 2000 this is expected to increase to 61 percent. The proportion who are women is even greater in the oldest group: among those over 85, 72 percent are women. This proportion is still higher among the widowed over 65: about 83% are women (Schick, 1986). The effects on ageism of this increasing proportion who are women are unclear, but it may increase the stereotype that most aged are frail old women.

COMPETITION

We have seen how competition between older native workers and younger immigrant workers increased job discrimination at the turn of the century. These days there is a different kind of competition that threatens to increase ageism: the competition for public funds, and especially for health care dollars.

One implication of the demographic trends described above is that more and more of the federal budget will have to be devoted to elders just to finance the existing programs in the future. The author of the quotation at the beginning of this chapter ("guns vs. canes") estimates that about half of the total federal budget will have to go to those 65 and over in 2025 (assuming that the federal budget is limited to the present 20% of gross national product) (Torrey, 1982). This would clearly require cutting some other major expenditures, such as the military. Alternately, if we wanted to maintain the present proportion of the budget going to elders (17%), we would have to increase the total federal budget to 27 percent of the gross national product.

Clearly such a budget squeeze could trigger a conflict between generations as to how much of the federal budget (and other public resources) should go to elders. Governor Richard Lamm of Colorado has already asserted that too much technology and money is being spent on the elderly population during their last years in comparison to the young, who have their entire lives before them (ABC's *Nightline*, April 4, 1984). Similarly, the president of the Population Association of America has asserted that there is a direct competition between the young and the old for society's resources: "Whereas expenditure on the elderly can be thought of mainly as consumption, expenditures on the young are a combination of consumption and investment" (Preston, 1984, p. 44).

Senator David Durenburger (Minn.) and Representative James Jones (Okla.) founded Americans for Generational Equity (AGE), which questions the future of the $200 billion Social Security system and the assumption that the young should support the old. This organization had over 800 members and a budget of $286,000 in 1987.

Fortunately, however, there is little evidence so far that such a conflict between generations is widespread. Public opinion polls consistently show as much or more support among those under 65 as among those over 65 for Social Security benefits and Medicare and other programs for elders (Harris, 1981; Kingson, Hirshorn, & Cornman, 1986). Most people under 65 perceive that their own long-term interest is involved in programs for elders; and they understand that if these programs did not exist, they would have to care for older relatives themselves.

OBSOLESCENCE

Earlier we mentioned that modernization theory posits that rapidly changing technology and new occupations make the job skills of older workers obsolete. This is particularly true if little is done to reeducate and keep up-to-date workers' skills and professionals' knowledge. The health professions now recognize that continuing education is necessary to keep their knowledge and skills up-to-date. Some companies do a limited amount of job retraining when technologies change. In Japan, most corporations put an emphasis on continuing reeducation and retraining of their workers to keep them from becoming obsolete.

But in general, Americans tend to assume that older workers will retire as soon as possible so that their retraining is not necessary or worthwhile. Job training programs tend to give preference to younger trainees. Most of our educational system is focused on younger people. Although some colleges, especially state colleges and universities, have reduced or free tuition programs for retired persons, and there are some innovative programs for older learners, these are exceptions rather than the rule.

Our general neglect of continuing education for older workers and retirees tends to hasten their obsolescence.

VALUE CONFLICT

We might expect that there would be large differences between the values of older and younger people for two reasons. The effects of aging might make older people emphasize different values. For example, because they do not have children of school age and are not expected to further their own education, they might deemphasize the value of education. Or elders might value accomplishments more than ambition because elders usually have accomplished more than the young.

A second reason for value differences between the generations is the "cohort effect": differences produced by being socialized in a different era (Palmore, 1978b). For example, older people might value family ties more than younger people, because the older generation was socialized when family ties were considered more important than they are today. This cohort effect is the cause of the stereotype that older people are "old-fashioned."

However, it is possible that a greater emphasis on family ties might be brought about by the effects of aging, such as retirement, which allows more time for family interests. Thus the effects of aging may work separately from cohort effects, or the two effects may reinforce each other. Whatever the reason, such differences in values could produce value conflict between elders and the younger generations. Such value conflict would tend to create ageism— in both the younger and older generations.

There has been considerable research and even more speculation about the "generation gap." This usually refers to the differences between youth and their parents. Differences between middle-aged persons and *their* parents have not been investigated as much. It seems reasonable that the generation gap would persist into old age—or even become widened.

To what extent does the research support such assumptions about generation gaps and value conflicts? Generally speaking, there is surprisingly little conflict between the generations. Rokeach (1973) found that out of 36 values, which people of all ages ranked, only 3 showed large age differences: people over 60 tended to rank a "comfortable life" higher than other people did, and people over 70 tended to rank "wisdom" and "responsibility" *lower* than other people did!

It seems understandable that older people would rank a comfortable life higher because that fits the situation of the average retired person. However, it is surprising that they would rank "wisdom" and "responsibility" lower. Perhaps older people rank them lower because they feel they have achieved these values and they are no longer so important; whereas younger people are less likely to feel they have achieved such values.

Whatever the explanation, the important point for our purposes is that there tended to be agreement among all ages as to the relative worth of most basic values. Furthermore, there was little change in values over time for those over age 30 (Rokeach, 1978). Thus, this research indicates that value conflict is not a major source of ageism between the generations.

Other researchers, such as Harris (1975, 1981), have also found basic agreement between the generations on such issues as mandatory retirement, government programs for elders, increasing Social Security taxes if necessary, and family support for elders. Similarly, elders tend to have political preferences and voting patterns in about the same proportions as younger people (Atchley, 1987b).

It is true that there are numerous political pressure groups, such as the Gray Panthers, the National Council of Senior Citizens, and the American Association of Retired Persons (see Chapters 9 and 14). But so far, they have been successful in getting legislation passed only for those programs that enjoy broad support among all age groups.

Similarly, one might expect that conflict between generations may become exacerbated in the future as the goal of reducing budget deficits collides with the goal of maintaining income supports, health care, and long-term care for elders. But so far, this has not become a serious conflict.

In summary, there appears to be little value conflict at present between elders and younger generations.

SEGREGATION

In race relations, segregation tends to breed suspicion, misunderstanding, stereotyping, and discrimination. This is the basis for the extensive legislation and judicial decisions prohibiting segregation on the basis of race.

In relations between age groups, the nature of segregation is rather different and its effects are debatable. Geographically, those over 65 are somewhat concentrated in Florida (18%), some Midwestern states like Arkansas and Iowa (14% each), and some Northeastern states like Pennsylvania and Rhode Island (14% each). On the other hand, there are less aged in some Western states like Utah and Wyoming (8% each). Alaska, as our "last frontier," has the least (3%). But most states have proportions of aged near the national average (12%) (U.S. Senate Special Committee on Aging, 1988).

Within the states, older people are more likely than those under 65 to live outside metropolitan areas, especially in small towns. Those who do live in metropolitan areas are more likely than those under 65 to live in the central cities. But the differences in these comparisons are relatively small, less than 5 percent.

Thus, there is little age segregation in terms of large geographical areas. There is more age segregation on a neighborhood basis where retirement communities have developed or special housing for the aged has been built. In both these cases, the segregation keeps younger people out, rather than forcing old people to live there. Most elderly residents say they prefer to live in such communities. They report that it is easier to make friends and they like the special facilities and the greater quiet in these communities (Bultena & Wood, 1969). Rosow (1967) found that aged living in an age-segregated apartment building were more likely to form friendships there than those living in age-integrated buildings.

On the other hand, there is some evidence that many older people do not want and would not benefit from age-segregated housing (Carp, 1975). Furthermore, even if some elders feel more comfortable in age-segregated housing, it may contribute to ageism nevertheless. As Barrow and Smith (1979) point out:

If young people never get to know old people, prejudice and discrimination against the elderly will continue. Growth and aging are both a part of life. To understand both and to see both happening are perhaps the fullest ways to experience living. . . . The aged, who feel rejected by the young, seek to find acceptance only among other aged and thereby segregate themselves from the young, who in turn reject elders more because they have no close contacts with them. (p. 220)

On the other hand, age-segregated housing may tend to produce feelings of group pride among elders and therefore higher self-esteem. This, in turn, would tend to reduce ageism. These arguments are similar to the arguments for and against (voluntary) racial segregation in neighborhoods, churches, clubs, and so on. The net effect of age-segregation on ageism is unknown and needs to be studied.

SELF-FULFILLING PROPHECY

Another well known source of racism is the self-fulfilling prophecy (Merton, 1968). This is the prophecy or belief that influences behavior in ways that tend to make the prophecy come true. A classic example is the belief that Blacks are less intelligent and do poorly in school. This belief causes discrimination in education against Blacks. As a result, many Blacks end up not doing well in school.

The process of the self-fulfilling prophecy derives from a basic theorem formulated by W. I. Thomas: "If men define situations as real, they are real in their consequences" (quoted by Merton, 1968). Self-fulfilling prophecies work the same way for or against the aged. If people believe elders cannot do any physically or mentally demanding work, they will force them to retire from such jobs and will not hire older workers for such jobs. As a result, elders end up not doing any demanding work.

For another example, if people believe that elders have no sexual capacity or desire, they will discourage elders in various ways from seeking or engaging in sexual activity. Cases have been reported in which children sought to have their aged parents committed to a mental hospital because they were living with members of the opposite sex (Lobsenz, 1974). As a result there is a reduction in the level of sexual activity that otherwise would be regarded as normal and healthy.

This process is particularly insidious when the victims of the prejudice come to believe it themselves. Many older people have been taught that sex is exclusively for the young, and so they are hesitant to admit having sexual motives and they feel guilty, ashamed, or embarrassed about engaging in sexual relations (Starr & Werner, 1961; Rubin, 1968).

To cite an example of a positive self-fulfilling prophecy, if people believe that older persons are better then younger persons in public office, they will tend to support older candidates for office. As a result, older persons will end up getting elected and doing better in public office.

DOUBLE JEOPARDY

The hypothesis of double jeopardy states that there is an *interaction* (or multiplicative) effect produced by the combination of any two minority statuses, such that the combined effect is greater than the addition of the two separate effects (Markides, 1987; Dowd & Bengston, 1978). For example, the double jeopardy hypothesis would state that differences between Blacks and whites are greater in old age than in middle age; or that differences between elders and nonaged are greater among Blacks than among whites.

The theory behind this hypothesis is that prejudice and discrimination against one minority group (such as Blacks) becomes greatly intensified when it is combined with the prejudice against another group (such as elders). If Blacks are perceived as having lower intelligence, then old Blacks are perceived as having almost no intelligence. Therefore, Blacks get less education in general and old Blacks get almost no education. If women are perceived as generally weaker, then old women are perceived as being completely helpless. Therefore, women get less stressful jobs and old women get almost no jobs.

However, various tests of this hypothesis which have used social indicators such as income, education, and so on have had mixed results. Dowd and Bengtson (1978) found some support for the hypothesis in their Los Angeles study; but Markides (1983) using national data did not find any such effect. If anything, his analysis tended to counter the double jeopardy hypothesis. Palmore and Manton (1973) found conflicting effects, depending on the type of minority groups combined: racial inequality in income was greater in old age, but gender inequality in income was less in old age.

Although I know of little statistical evidence, there seems to be agreement among most observers that there is a "double standard of aging" applied to men and women in regard to such things as beauty (handsomeness), sexuality, and competence (Hodge, 1987; Sontag, 1972). Women are generally regarded as losing their beauty, sexuality, and competence at an earlier age than men. Many older men are regarded as still handsome, sexually attractive, and highly competent; few older women are.

Thus, the hypothesis of double jeopardy appears to be true only in certain combinations with certain variables, but not generally true. Other factors must be taken into account to understand how and when double jeopardy operates.

SUMMARY

The processes of modernization contribute to negative ageism by creating a greater supply of older persons than the society needs, by making their job skills obsolete, by increasing retirement, by undercutting their prestige as sources of knowledge, and by leaving elders behind in rural and deteriorated areas.

However, these effects may be counteracted by a tradition of respect for the elderly, and the status of elders may now be increasing in postindustrial societies.

The few aged in Colonial times usually enjoyed an advantaged position because of their power in the major institutions of that day. After the Revolutionary War, new equalitarian ideologies tended to undercut the advantages of elders. After the Civil War, rapid modernization encouraged the growth of negative ageism. Increased competition from younger immigrants also contributed to more ageism.

During and after World War II, several developments began to improve the status of elders: the labor shortage during the war, the improvement in retirement income, and the initiation of several major federal programs including prohibition of discrimination in employment.

The major demographic trends affecting elders were the rapid increase in the number and proportion of elderly in society, especially of the very old, and the increasing proportion of women among the elderly. The net effects of these trends on ageism are unclear at present. One effect is clear, however: the increasing aged population is increasing competition for federal funds.

Workers' skills tend to become obsolete as they age in our society, because we do not emphasize continuing education and retraining as much as some societies do. This obsolescence is both a result and cause of negative ageism.

There is surprisingly little value conflict between the generations and what conflict there is does not appear to be a major source of ageism. There seems to be growing segregation of elders in retirement communities, apartment buildings, and certain sections of the country. However, most of this segregation is voluntary and there are some benefits from it that may tend to offset its contribution to negative ageism.

Self-fulfilling prophecies based on negative stereotypes of aged tend to increase discrimination and hurt elders. This is especially insidious when elders themselves believe the negative stereotypes and therefore behave in ways that tend to confirm the stereotypes.

Various investigations of the double jeopardy theory of aging produce conflicting results. In certain respects there is even *more* equality between minority and majority groups among the aged than among the nonaged.

Thus, there are many social influences on ageism, although some potential influences appear to have little impact. We now turn to a description of various ways in which the culture supports the individual and social influences on ageism.

6

Cultural Sources

The culture treats the old like the fag end of what was once good material.
                                                                    Max Lerner, 1957.

Humans are obsessed with aging. They'd do anything to avoid it.
                        The Alien Nation (TV series, September 25, 1989)

You're not getting older—you're getting better.
                        Husband to wife in a commercial for hand lotion.

There are many aspects of our culture that support ageism. In fact our culture is so permeated with ageism, and we are so conditioned by it, that we are often unaware of it. Yet our culture encourages ageism through "blaming the victim," and through our values, language, humor, songs, art, literature, television, and cultural lag.

BLAMING THE VICTIM

There is a well-known tendency in minority relations for the oppressors to blame their victims for their oppression, thereby absolving themselves from guilt (Levin & Levin, 1980; see also Chapter 3 above). It was said that Blacks needed to be enslaved because they were incapable of civilized behavior if free. Later it was said that Blacks should be kept in menial positions because they were incapable of higher intelligence and responsibility. Poor people are blamed for their poverty because of low intelligence, lack of morals, and laziness. Women were denied the vote because they were incapable of rational choice. Even today victims of rape are often blamed because they are said to have been provocative and have "asked for it."

In our modern culture elders may be blamed for the discrimination against them by the use of negative stereotypes: they may be forced to retire because of the beliefs that they tend to be sick, senile, and incapable. Government agencies may discriminate against them because of the beliefs that they do not need rehabilitation, education, mental health services, and so on as much as younger people. Families may abuse and neglect older members because of the beliefs that they are senile, ugly, unpleasant, and useless. Health care is scarce because many health care professionals think older patients are ugly, unpleasant, demanding, difficult, and unrewarding. Older patients may be unnecessarily forced into institutions because relatives believe it would be too difficult or unpleasant to care for them at home, or think they are incapable of taking care of themselves safely.

Blaming the victim is often an unconscious process. It is often perpetuated by well-meaning and sincere people who think that discrimination against the victims is necessary "for their own good," or "for the good of society." This process is similar to the process of rationalization discussed in Chapter 4.

VALUES

A *value* is anything that is prized or thought to be beneficial. A *cultural value* may be defined as a widely held belief or sentiment that some activities, relationships, feelings, or goals are important to the community's identity or well-being (Broom & Selznick, 1968) A society's *value orientations* are the basic values that underlie its social structure and expectations about behavior.

Robin Williams produced the classic summary of eight major value orientations in the United States (Williams, 1960). Five of these values tend to support ageism.

1. *Active mastery* rather than *passive acceptance*. Insofar as elders are perceived as more passive and accepting, they appear to deviate from this value orientation.
2. Concern with the *external world* rather than with *inner experience*. Since elders are usually perceived as more concerned with the inner experience of meaning and affect, and more contemplative about self and personal history (reminiscing, writing memoirs, etc.) they appear to deviate from this value orientation.
3. *Rationalism* rather than *traditionalism*. Because elders are perceived as more traditional, past-oriented, and conservative, rather than rational, future-oriented, and favoring change, they appear to deviate from this value orientation.
4. *Universalism* rather than *particularism*. Insofar as elders are perceived as more concerned with special treatment of relatives, friends, or other particular types of people, rather than with uniform rules or principles (such as equality before the law and equal opportunity regardless of sex, race, etc.), they appear to deviate from this value orientation.
5. Concern with *horizontal* rather than *vertical* relationships. If elders are perceived as more concerned with superordinate-subordinate relations (such as to children and servants) rather than with peer relations (such as siblings and co-workers); and more concerned with hierarchy rather than equality, they appear to deviate from this value orientation.

These apparent deviations by elders from the basic value orientations in our society tend to support prejudice and discrimination against them. Condemnation of such deviation is summed up in such terms as "old fashioned," "old fogy," "out of date," and "stick-in-the-mud."

Rokeach (1973) did a comprehensive survey of men and women over age 18 in the United States to determine their most important personal values. Among the most important *outcome* values for both men and women were family security, freedom, a comfortable life, happiness, and equal opportunity. Insofar as aging is perceived as threatening family security, freedom, a comfortable life, and happiness (because of disability, dependency, reduced income, and senility) aging is viewed negatively. If elders are perceived as opposed to equal opportunity (because of racism, sexism, and other forms of particularism), they appear to threaten a basic American value.

Similarly, among the most important *instrumental* values were ambition (hard-working, aspiring), competence (competitive), and independence (self-reliant, self-sufficient). Because elders are usually perceived as being less ambitious, competent, and independent, they appear to have less of our most valued qualities. These perceptions also support negative ageism.

LANGUAGE

One of the most subtle but pervasive influences of culture on our attitudes is our language: the words we use to identify or describe a person or group; the derivations, definitions, and connotations of these words; their synonyms and antonyms, and the context in which they are used. Our language often supports ageism in all of these ways. There is considerable evidence that our language influences our perceptions and prejudices (Berelson & Steiner, 1964; Palmore, 1962).

Covey (1988) analyzed English terms for older people throughout history and found that these terms reflected the "decline in status of the elderly and the increased focus on the debilitative effects of aging" (p. 297). He also found that terms for old women have a much longer history of negative connotations than those for old men because women not only faced a long history of ageism, but also sexism and religious persecution.

Webster's Dictionary (1987) shows that the etymology of *old* has positive connotations: it is akin to the Latin *alere* (to nourish), *alescere* (to grow), and *altus* (high, deep). Furthermore, of the 17 meanings, 13 are neutral *(ancient, of long standing, advanced in years)* or positive *(venerable, experienced)*. However, 4 meanings have negative connotations: *showing the effects of time or use: worn; no longer vigorous, no longer in use: discarded, obsolete;* and *showing the characteristics of age (looked old at 20)*.

Webster's Thesaurus (Laird, 1985) lists 75 synonyms for the two meanings that apply to old people or things. Of these synonyms, the following 57 are usually negative:

(No longer vigorous) past one's prime, debilitated, infirm, inactive, deficient, enfeebled, decrepit, exhausted, tired, impaired, anemic, broken down, wasted, doddering, senile, on the shelf, ancient, gone to seed, with one foot in the grave and the other on a banana peel.

(Worn) time-worn, worn-out, thin, patched, ragged, faded, used, in holes, rubbed off, mended, broken-down, fallen to pieces, tumbled down, fallen in, given way, long used, out of use, rusted, crumbled, past usefulness, dilapidated, weather-beaten, ramshackle, battered, shattered, shabby, castoff, decayed, antiquated, decaying, stale, useless, tattered, in rags, torn, moth-eaten.

Only 3 synonyms are positive: *venerable, matured, seasoned.* Thus the majority of synonyms for *old* as applied to people or things are negative, a few are positive, and the rest are neutral or ambiguous (*aged, elderly, gray,* etc.).

There are 50 combinations of *old* with other words or endings (Webster, 1987). Of these, most are neutral, and 3 are usually positive (*old Glory, old hand,* and *old master*), but 7 are usually negative (*old-fangled, old-fashioned, old guard, old hat, old maid, old Nick,* and *old wives' tales*).

When we look at the opposite of *old,* namely *young* and *youthful,* most definitions appear neutral *(being in the first or early stage of life),* but one is negative *(having little experience)* and 2 are usually positive (*new,* and *fresh, vital or vigorous*).

Thus, words like *old* and *young* do not necessarily have negative definitions or connotations; but many of them tend to support ageism.

Nuessel (1982) has done an analysis of the language used to depict elders and found it to be "overwhelmingly negative in scope." He also found that many ageist terms are doubly offensive because they contain both ageist and sexist references *(biddy, crone, hag, old maid).*

Many negative adjectives do not specifically refer to elders, but are often associated with being old, such as *cantankerous, constipated, cranky, crotchety, eccentric, feebleminded, frumpy, garrulous, grumpy, over-age, peevish, rambling, toothless, withered, wizened,* and *wrinkled.*

Even the adjective *retired* may have negative connotations because of its alternate meanings of *withdrawn* or *gone to bed.* As a result, some retired elders try to counteract this connotation by saying they are "actively retired," "partially retired," or "retired but busier than ever."

There is a more basic and subtle way in which our language encourages ageism. That is the equating of chronological age with various positive or negative characteristics. For example, the phrase *young at heart* means alert, active, vigorous, fresh, innovative, and fun-loving—all positive characteristics. The implication, of course, is that the "old at heart" are dull, passive, slow, stale, old-fashioned, and wet blankets. Similarly, a "youthful figure" is one that is trim, beautiful, and attractive. By implication an "old figure" would be fat, ugly, and unattractive.

There are numerous examples of such equations. "Youthful skin" means skin that is unblemished, unwrinkled, soft, and smooth. "Aged skin" means blemished, wrinkled, rough, dry, and bumpy. To "stay young" means to stay healthy, alert, vigorous, active, and beautiful; by implication, to "grow old" means to become unhealthy, senile, weak, passive, and ugly. A "young heart" means one that is healthy and strong; an "old heart" means one that is diseased and weak. The reader may think of other examples of such equations.

It seems that chronological age terms often become euphemisms or code words for positive or negative characteristics that one does not want to name overtly. Apparently people often think it would be more polite or tactful to use "old" or "aging" rather than the real meaning of decrepit, senile, withered, or ugly. The problem is that using "old" or "aging" as euphemisms for negative characteristics tends to reinforce the stereotype that most old people have these negative characteristics.

To avoid such ageist language one could avoid the use of chronological age terms *(young, youthful, old, aged)* when the real meaning is some positive or negative physical, mental, or social characteristic *(frail, senile,* or *obsolete)*. Instead of "youthful skin" one could specify unwrinkled, unblemished, or beautiful skin. Instead of "youthful figure," one could specify trim or attractive. Instead of "stay young" one could say "stay healthy, alert, vigorous, active," and so on. (see Chapter 12).

A similar semantic pattern is the linking of "old" with some negative trait by using "and." Common linkages are "old and senile," "old and frail," "old and poor," "old and lonely," "old and depressed," and so on. Why are such linkages so common? Perhaps the assumption is that the "old" explains the negative trait (which of course it does not), or that the negative trait is especially problematic when one is old, or that most old people have the trait (which they do not). Whatever the explanation, such semantic linkage tends to reinforce the negative stereotypes of ageism.

The equating of old age and disability is illustrated by a recent study of professionals between 50 and 60 (Karp, 1988). Karp found that these professionals "see middle age as ending and old age as beginning when they become physically impaired" (p. 730). This

explains the "paradox" that many of them experienced: the contradiction between the way they felt and their chronological age.
They actually felt fine physically and mentally, but they (and the
rest of society) assumed that someone their age should feel more
impaired or debilitated.

Barbato & Feezel (1987) recently did a study of attitudes toward
different terms for aging among different age groups. They found
that the most preferred terms in all age groups were *mature American, senior citizen,* and *retired person.* All age groups also tended to
agree that *aged, elderly,* and *old (anything)* were negative terms.

As indicated in Chapter 1, I prefer to use the term *elder* because
of its positive connotations of one having authority or prestige
because of age and experience (Webster, 1987). *Elderly* often has
some negative connotations of declining or frail.

HUMOR AND SONGS

In 1971 I published the first study of attitudes toward aging as
shown by humor. This was a content analysis of 264 jokes about
aging and elders, classified in terms of subject matter, gender,
activity, and positive versus negative view of aging. More than half
of the jokes reflected a negative view of aging or elders, and only
one-quarter were clearly positive toward aging (see Appendix B for
some examples).

Since then several other studies (Davies, 1977; Demos & Jache,
1981; Dillon & Jones, 1981; Polisar, 1982; Richman, 1977; Smith,
1979) have done content analyses of jokes, cartoons, and birthday
cards about aging. They all reached similar conclusions: that the
majority of this humor reflects or supports negative attitudes
toward aging, and that positive humor about aging is rare.

Even jokes that are judged to be "positive" often depend on a
contradiction of negative stereotypes for their humor. For example,

> One old lady tells her friend, "I didn't sleep well last night because a
> man kept pounding on my door."
> "Why didn't you open the door?"
> "What, and let him out?"

This is funny only because of the stereotype that assumes old
ladies are not interested in sex. Thus, even "positive" jokes often
assume negative stereotypes.

In summary, most humor about aging tends to support negative ageism. Just as there are racist and sexist jokes, there are ageist jokes. Most of the tellers and listeners are probably not conscious of their ageist implications. This may even increase the joke's impact on the listener's unconscious attitudes.

Similarly, a recent analysis of over 300 pieces of sheet music related to aging found that a substantial majority present a negative view of aging and old age (Cohen & Kruschwitz, 1990).

ART

The images of elders presented in visual art in the United States have changed markedly throughout our history (Achenbaum & Kusnerz, 1978). From the Revolutionary War to the Civil War, most elders were given special respect for their valuable contributions to the new nation and as custodians of virtue. This respect was reflected in the art (McKee & Kauppinen, 1987), woodcarvings, and daguerreotypes of the period (Achenbaum & Kusnerz, 1978). But toward the end of this period, more negative views are reflected in some art, such as the lithographs of "The Life and Age of Man" and "The Life and Age of Woman" by James Baille printed in 1848 (Achenbaum & Kusnerz, 1978). These lithographs show both man and woman as rapidly declining in health and abilities after age 70 until they are pitiful figures at ages 90 and 100.

After the Civil War, with the growth of mass production, mass education, medical, and other sciences, more negative images began to predominate. These include images of disease, "the dirty old man," eccentricity, uselessness, loneliness, unemployment, and poverty (Achenbaum & Kusnerz, 1978).

After the establishment of Social Security in 1934, images of elders began to be more positive, along with substantial improvements in their economic and physical health. These images include more healthy, productive, useful, happy, prosperous, creative, politically active, and even sexually active elders (Achenbaum & Kusnerz, 1978). Of course many negative images also persist.

Thus art has had a variable influence on ageism: first encouraging positive attitudes, then negative, and recently more positive attitudes.

LITERATURE

Like art, literary images of old age present considerable variety. One analysis of 87 novels published between 1950 and 1975 that describe old age from the point of view of a person over 60 years old, found that about 40 percent dealt with some problem of elders such as institutionalization, isolation, segregation, and the power struggle between the older and younger generations (Sohngen, 1977). Presumably the other 60 percent presented more neutral or positive images of old age.

Similarly, an analysis of 9 contemporary novels found that they challenge the myth of sexlessness in elders and "extend to the elderly the liberal sexual attitudes which other segments of the population have been experiencing" (Loughman, 1980, p. 182).

An analysis of 120 poems by contemporary American poets age 60 and over found that about two-thirds dealt with problems or were mainly negative toward old age (Clark, 1980). The other third depict aging as continued growth; old age as a time of vision, wisdom, and stature; or of continuing and deepening love. The author concludes: "That so many of the poems value continued struggle, change, growth, and self-realization in old age leads me to think that there runs, somewhere, a great river of strength among our elders" (p. 191).

Thus, contemporary literature presents a mixture of negative and positive images of aging. To the extent that they reflect simplistic stereotypes, they reinforce ageism. To the extent that they deal with realistic individual problems and potentials, they undermine ageism.

CHILDREN'S LITERATURE

Literature written for children may be even more important than that written for adults in terms of shaping attitudes toward aging and elders, because it affects attitudes during the early formative years. It is surprising to find that older characters in children's books tend to be portrayed in a positive way (Robin, 1977). (The old witches are exceptions.) Furthermore, the illustrations tend to present attractive, healthy older people (Storck & Cutler, 1977).

Seltzer and Atchley (1971) analyzed children's books from the past 100 years and concluded that there were few negative attitudes shown toward old people. Furthermore, there was little change in these attitudes and positive attitudes predominated throughout the 100 years.

It is true that the older characters tend to be undeveloped and peripheral (Peterson & Eden, 1977; Peterson & Karnes, 1976), but this is not surprising when we recognize that the main characters in children's literature tend to be children (Atchley, 1988). Ansello (1977) concluded that older characters come off negatively not in content but because of their blandness; older characters were poorly developed and old age seemed boring. But this hardly seems to be an adequate explanation for the development of ageism among children.

How, then, can we account for the widespread ageism that has been found among children (Seefeldt, Jantz, Galpem, & Serock, 1977; Hickey et al., 1968; Hickey & Kalish, 1968)? Apparently it must be absorbed from other sources, such as parents and teachers, television, and songs.

TELEVISION

This is the most important mass medium in U.S. society (and in most of the rest of the world). Americans watch television more than three hours a day on average, and it is the leading pastime of middle-aged and older Americans (Moss & Lawton, 1982; Pfeiffer & Davis, 1971).

There are several ways in which television supports ageism. First, there are few elder characters portrayed in prime time programs (6% according to Ansello, 1978) and in children's Saturday programs (2% of human characters, 7% of cartoon characters according to Jantz, Seefeldt, Cunningham, and Serock, 1978). Soap operas are the exception: almost 16 percent of the characters were judged to be age 60 or over. When elders are absent or rare, it may send the message that elders are unimportant or uninteresting.

Secondly, there is a sexist bias among the elders that are portrayed. Only 10 percent of the people on TV over 65 are female (Davis & Davis, 1985), and those few older women are apt to be portrayed negatively (Gerbner, Grass, Signorielli, & Morgan, 1980). Older women tend to be comic or eccentric figures and likely to be treated disrespectfully. In contrast, older men are given increased sexual attractiveness as they age, often based on their increased social power.

However, there are some recent exceptions to this negative image of older women, such as in *The Golden Girls*, *Murder She Wrote*, and also in recent soap operas where they are often seen as official and informal advisors (Elliott, 1984). Nevertheless, older women are more often seen as the nurturer, adoring attendant, or nag, than in other roles.

Third, elders in nighttime television series were found to be usually "bad guys," prone to failure, and generally unhappy (Aronoff, 1974). Another study found that older characters were rated as less attractive, sociable, warm, and intelligent compared to younger characters. On the other hand, one study found that over half of elders were presented in a favorable light (Petersen, 1973). This discrepancy between studies is probably due to differences in methods of analysis and sampling, as well as to possible bias in the observers.

Again there have been several recent exceptions to the past negative image of elders in nighttime television, such as the older characters in *Dynasty* and *In the Heat of the Night*.

Fourth, television's portrayal of elders in news and documentary programming tends to be negative. The elders in the news usually have some serious problem or have suffered some disaster that is the basis for human interest or commentary (Atchley, 1988).

Fifth, elders in commercials are less likely to be physically active and more likely to have health problems than younger people (Harris & Feinberg, 1977). Elders are overrepresented in commercials for health aids, and totally absent from commercials for clothing, appliances, cars, and cleaning products. This supports the stereotype that most elders are inactive and sick.

On the other hand, public affairs and talk shows generally present elders positively (Harris & Feinberg, 1977). Elders on these shows tend to be influential business leaders or politicians, or respected actors or artists.

In summary, the images of elders presented on television tend to be clusters of stereotypes, sometimes positive, more often negative, but usually simplistic (Davis, 1987). There is some evidence that television is moving toward more representative and accurate portrayals of elders (Atchley, 1988). But it appears that, at least in the past, television has been a major source of ageism in our society.

CULTURAL LAG

This has been defined as "A situation in which some parts of a culture (usually material culture) change at a faster rate than other parts (usually nonmaterial)" (Broom & Selznick, 1968, p. 638). A current example would be our recent pollution of the atmosphere so as to reduce the ozone layer. Our culture is just beginning to develop laws and international agreements to deal with that change in our "material culture."

The problem of ageism is partly a result of cultural lag. Two or three generations ago the majority of people over 65 probably did fit one or more of the stereotypes about elders: they probably were sick, senile, poor, isolated, and/or unhappy. Most people did not even live to age 65, and those few who did, tended to die within a few years.

Since then the health, mental abilities, financial security, social activity, and life satisfaction of elders has improved markedly. Most no longer fit any of the old negative stereotypes. But most people have not heard the good news, and even among those who have heard, old attitudes and habits resist change.

Thus ageism is partly a hangover from a previous era when such negative views of elders were more realistic. The optimistic implication of this is that when people find out the good news about the improvements among elders, they will begin to reduce their ageism. Unfortunately there are many other personal, social, and cultural sources of ageism that are more difficult to change.

SUMMARY

Ageism permeates our culture so thoroughly and conditions our attitudes and perceptions so much that most of us are unaware of most of the ageism in it.

The process of "blaming the victim" is often used to justify the discrimination against elders. Negative stereotypes are used to blame elders for the discrimination against them by employers, government agencies, families, health care institutions, and the public.

Several of the major value orientations of our culture tend to support negative ageism: active mastery, external world, rationalism, universalism, and vertical relationships. Aging may be perceived as threatening important outcome values in our culture such as family security, freedom, a comfortable life, happiness, and equal opportunity. Elders may also be perceived as having less of the important instrumental values such as being ambitious, capable, and independent.

Our language tends to support negative ageism through negative connotations of *old* and positive connotations of *young*. Our language often equates old age with various negative characteristics, such as decline and deterioration; while young age is equated with positive characteristics such as health and beauty.

The majority of humor, songs, and art tend to support negative ageism. Literature and television present a variety of images of elders, but television has been more negative than positive in the past. TV appears to be moving toward more representative and accurate portrayals of elders.

Having seen how our culture contributes to ageism, we now turn to the consequences of ageism in our society.

7

Consequences

Old men have lived many years; they have often been fooled and often made mistakes; and life on the whole is a bad business. The result is that they are sure about nothing and under-do everything. They are cynical; that is, they put the worst construction on everything. They are small minded, because they have been humbled by life: their desires are set upon nothing more exalted than what will help them keep alive.
Aristotle (McKee, 1982)

Ageism, like all prejudices, influences the behavior of its victims.
Butler, 1987

GAINS FROM NEGATIVE AGEISM

Simpson and Yinger, in their classic text on racism (1985) state: "It seems unlikely that human beings would show such an enormous capacity for prejudice and discrimination were it not for the gains they seem to acquire" (p. 156). This applies to ageism as well as to racism. Negative ageism provides numerous personal gains to younger people.

There are obvious gains to younger workers from employment discrimination against older workers (Palmore, 1972c). Refusing to hire and promote older workers means more jobs and promotions for younger workers. Compulsory retirement for older workers opens up jobs for younger workers and reduces unemployment among younger workers.

Discrimination against older workers can also provide some benefits for employers. They can reduce wages by hiring lower-paid younger workers to replace higher-paid older workers. Employers may also save the costs of providing pensions to their retired workers if they get rid of the older workers before they become eligible for pensions. Compulsory retirement by age also avoids the embarrassment and difficulties of evaluating the abilities of older workers and forcing the less able to retire.

As noted in Chapter 6, disengagement theory argues that retirement from work and other roles benefits society because disengagement allows smoother and more predictable transitions of roles from older to younger workers. A counterargument to this theory is that smooth transitions in critical jobs can usually be achieved by increasing the incentives for voluntary retirement rather than forcing retirement.

Butler (1987) argues that ageism can provide psychological gains to younger people:

> Ageism allows the younger generation to see older people as different from themselves; thus, they suddenly cease to identify with their elders as human beings and thereby reduce their own sense of fear and dread of aging, illness, and death. (p. 22)

He also argues that ageism becomes a method of avoiding society's responsibility toward elders. This would be a gain for younger persons because it would reduce the costs of providing support and care for elders.

Certainly elder abuse and neglect may occur because proper care of disabled elders may be expensive in both money and time. In pathological cases, elder abuse may satisfy sadistic impulses or the desire for revenge against parents or other authority figures.

Limiting or neglecting health care of elders also can save large amounts of money and professional time, as discussed in Chapter 11. It could also reduce the health professional's frustration when faced with the complex and difficult medical problems that elders often present.

Simpson and Yinger (1985) point out the prestige gains from racism:

> If a whole group of fellow human beings can be kept in an inferior position—and if I can persuade myself that they are really inferior—I can get a comfortable feeling of prestige that my own individual achievements might not command. (p. 157)

Similarly, if younger people can convince themselves that they are superior to older people, their self-esteem can be enhanced. This is a common motivation for ageism among those who feel personally inadequate or insecure (see Chapter 4).

Kearl (1982) claims that many elders also gain self-esteem from the negative stereotypes of elders, because they can perceive themselves as being relatively advantaged compared to the stereotype. Surveys of elders do indicate that the majority think most other elders are worse off than they themselves are (Harris, 1975).

GAINS FROM POSITIVE AGEISM

Just as negative ageism benefits younger persons, positive ageism provides some gains for older persons. Employment discrimination in favor of older workers by definition benefits the older workers. Federal programs, such as the Senior Community Service Employment Program, provide hundreds of millions of dollars for their older employees.

The billions of dollars given elders through the Social Security and other income transfer programs obviously benefit elders, but it is less obvious that most of this money comes out of the income of younger people. This is because the fiction is maintained that Social Security is like an annuity, in which you make "contributions" (pay taxes) while working, and then receive a pension after retirement.

In fact, Social Security is basically a pay-as-you-go income transfer program in which the average person receives much more than the value of their investment and interest. Many do not recognize that Social Security benefits to retired elders are balanced by the Social Security taxes paid by workers.

In 1989, for example, the trust funds for Social Security totaled about $40 billion, which would last only about 10 weeks if income stopped. Beginning in the early 1990s the Social Security trust funds will build up substantial balances, but these will decline and become exhausted by about 2060, according to the intermediate cost estimate (Myers, 1987).

Similarly, the billions of dollars enjoyed by elders in the form of tax breaks are balanced by the extra taxes that must be paid, mainly by younger people, to make up for these "tax expenditures." When the government sets up any special program restricted to older persons, such as senior centers and nutrition sites, only elders can benefit, while the bill is paid mostly by younger taxpayers.

When police, juries, and judges are more lenient with older offenders, the offender appears to be benefiting; but more equitable justice may be better for both society and the offender in the long run. When voters favor older candidates just because of their age, the older candidates benefit; but voting for the best candidate regardless of age would be more beneficial for society as a whole.

When elders exploit younger family members, they may believe that such benefits are due them as parents and elders. (There is a popular bumper sticker that reflects this view: "Live long enough to become a burden on your children!".) The difference between proper filial support and exploitation is debatable and depends on one's assumptions and point of view.

Clearly Medicare and Medicaid have been of great benefit to sick elders, especially low-income elders. These programs probably contributed to the decline in disability among elders since 1960 (Palmore, 1986a). But if Medicare were available to persons of all ages, many more people would have benefited from it.

Because of these gains to elders from positive ageism, most elders would probably oppose the reduction or elimination of such ageism. Professional providers of service to elders also oppose reductions in their programs for similar reasons of self-interest (Estes, 1979).

PERSONAL COSTS TO ELDERS

It is well known that victims of prejudice and discrimination tend to adopt the dominant group's negative image of the subordinate group and to behave in ways that conform to the negative image. This has occured among Blacks (Simpson & Yinger, 1985) and among women (Friedan, 1963). Similarly, elders tend to accept as many of the negative stereotypes about old age as do younger people (Palmore, 1988). These stereotypes include the assumptions that most aged are asexual, intellectually rigid, unproductive, ineffective, and disengaged. As a result, many aged tend to avoid sexual relations, avoid new ideas, avoid productivity, avoid effective activity, and avoid social engagement (Levin & Levin, 1980). This is an example of the "self-fulfilling prophecy":

Young people are socialized to accept negative age stereotypes. As a result, they discourage, even punish, any behavior on the part of elders that is active, effective, or competent. In turn elders come to accept the negative stereotypes and to act in accordance with the role of senior citizen. (Levin & Levin, 1980, p. 100)

Montague (1977) describes how this works:

Most older people have a way of acting as if they were older. They're playing a role. This role of elders has not only been imposed by others upon them, but is self-imposed. They think, "I'm this age, so I have to behave this way." They feel they must say, "Oh well, when you're my age . . ." or "When I was your age . . ." that sort of thing, to emphasize the fact that they're older. This perception of a difference between the old and the young comes not only from the young, but from the older person who, by his behavior, accepts the definition of being old. (p. 49)

Butler (1987) says that such conformity with negative stereotypes is a kind of "collaboration with the enemy," the ageism in our society. He reports that Margaret Thaler Singer observed similarities between the Rorschach test findings in a sample of healthy aged and a sample of American prisoners of war who collaborated with their captors in Korea.

Such conformity obviously has a cost in the loss of freedom to be sexually active, creative, productive, effective, and engaged. Such inactivity tends to form a vicious circle in which the inactivity causes atrophy of abilities, which in turn lead to even less activity. Thus, one of the costs of accepting these stereotypes is a more rapid deterioration than would be normal in a more active and engaged person.

Another cost of accepting such stereotypes is usually a loss of self-esteem and happiness. The high rate of suicide among older men may be one effect of such ageism.

A third cost of accepting these stereotypes is the fact that many elders fail to seek proper treatment for various medical and mental ailments because they think such ailments are a normal part of aging and nothing can be done about it. As a result, their ailments tend to get worse and to multiply until it is too late to do much about them.

Similarly, some elders accept being poor as an expected and normal part of being old, when their poverty is really due to their lack of saving, poor financial planning, or unwillingness to work in order to supplement their income.

On the other hand, denial of the realities of aging have their cost also. For example, those who attempt to deny their normal aging through face-lifts, hair dyes, and various cosmetics designed to conceal wrinkles, pay a stiff price for their denial. Such denial would be unnecessary if aging was not thought to be ugly and indicative of senility and senescence.

COSTS TO YOUNGER PERSONS

The costs of prejudice to the prejudiced person are uncertain and controversial. Simpson and Yinger (1985) assert, "The great interdependence of all people within a society . . . makes it impossible for a dominant group to inflict penalties on minority groups without being penalized itself. In the eloquent words of John Dunne, 'No man is an island' " (p. 158).

However, there have been no well-controlled studies of the effects of ageism on the ageist person and it is difficult to separate cause from effect. In other words, even if there are more personality problems among ageist persons, is this because the ageism caused the personality problems, or because the personality problems cause the ageism? Therefore, what follows are largely speculations derived from minority group theory, and these assumptions would need to be tested by research before we could assert them as facts.

By definition, prejudice is a categorical prejudgment of persons because they are classified as members of a particular group. To the extent that this prejudice is inaccurate, one of the inevitable effects is a loss of contact with reality. Rationality is contradicted by prejudice, which furnishes a greatly oversimplified or inaccurate explanation of one's difficulties. As a result, the actions that are supposed to solve the difficulties are ineffective and are unable to effect a real cure.

For example, when people use elders as a scapegoat for the Federal deficit rather than recognizing that the real causes were the tax cuts and the increases in military spending, they are unlikely to favor policies that will actually reduce the federal deficit (Binstock, 1983).

For another example, when people blame high unemployment on elders who continue to work and "take jobs away from young people," they are unlikely to favor policies that will effectively combat recession, inefficiency, negative balance of trade, and other more realistic causes of high unemployment.

In addition to such irrationality, there may be personal costs in terms of guilt, moral ambivalence, and the tension this produces.

Gunnar Myrdal in his classic, *An American Dilemma* (1944), pointed out the moral ambivalence produced by the conflict between democratic ideals versus discrimination against Blacks. There is a similar tension produced by the conflict between democratic ideals and ageism. This tension may not be consciously recognized, but may take its toll through vague feelings of guilt, discomfort, and tendencies toward victim blaming, projection, and authoritarian personalities. There is evidence that people who have more prejudice against elders tend to be prejudiced against other groups as well (Chapter 4).

ECONOMIC COSTS

The economic costs of ageism are difficult to calculate and the total depends on one's assumptions. However, a conservative estimate, based on the assumptions below, would be that the total costs are well over $178 billion per year.

The tax breaks for elderly (including exclusion of pension contribution and earnings) cost a total of $73 billion in 1985 (Hudson, 1987). It has been estimated that about one-half of such tax breaks go to middle class or affluent persons (those with $20,000 or more in 1982; Gary, 1987). If we assume that this half goes to aged people just because of their age rather than their need, we would estimate that $36.5 billion of the tax breaks represent a cost of positive ageism.

The Old Age and Survivors Insurance Program (part of Social Security) cost $162 billion in 1985 (Hudson, 1987). If we use the same assumption as for the tax breaks, we would estimate that $81 billion of this went to middle class and affluent elders because of age rather than need and therefore was another cost of positive ageism.

Medicare cost $63 billion in 1985 (Hudson, 1987). Using the same logic, we would estimate that about $31 billion of this went to those who could afford private health insurance and therefore represents a third cost of positive ageism.

It is more difficult to estimate the costs of negative ageism, such as lost productivity or retired workers who could and would contribute to the Gross National Product if there were no discrimination against them and they were encouraged to continue working. If we assumed that the three million workers over 65, who are presently in the labor market, could be doubled by equal opportunity and attractive wages, that would result in another three million experienced workers contributing to our productivity. If we estimated the value of their productivity at about $10,000 per worker (in 1990 dollars), this would amount to about $30 billion a year.

Adding together these estimates results in a total of $178 billion a year in economic costs of ageism. This figure does not include the many other special programs provided for elders under the Older Americans Act, Supplementary Security Income, Medicaid, public assistance, nor state and local programs for elders.

SOCIAL COSTS

The social costs of ageism are impossible to quantify. We can only outline the major types of social costs to older and younger people produced by ageism.

One of the largest costs to elders is the social isolation caused by residential segregation, disengagement of organizations and informal groups from elders, unnecessary institutionalization, and other forms of discrimination. Such isolation can be very costly in terms of the mental and physical illness it may produce or encourage, including a high rate of suicide among older men. Such isolation also deprives elders of the emotional support and enjoyment provided by normal social relations with younger people.

The costs to younger people would include the loss of the wisdom and guidance that elders have to offer; the loss of personal knowledge of what aging is really like, based on personal observations of the aging process; the development of unrealistic fears and prejudices about aging and death; the loss of knowledge about what the "olden days" were actually like, based on the personal experiences of older relatives and friends; and the loss of the warm emotional support and enjoyment that is provided by normal relations with older people.

We have mentioned as a personal cost the effects of using the aged as scapegoats for national problems such as unemployment, the Federal budget deficit, and the negative balance of trade. The scapegoating also has social costs because it leads to unrealistic social and political policies which not only fail to solve the basic problems, but may even increase problems (Binstock, 1983).

RESPONSES OF ELDERS

As we have seen, most Americans believe generally negative stereotypes about elders, which are the basis for generally negative expectations about the way they should and will behave. As Levin and Levin (1980) put it, Americans

> generally expect and even encourage elders to be asexual, intellectually rigid, unproductive, ineffective, and disengaged. Senior citizens are supposed to stay out of the way, sit in their rocking chairs, and enjoy the golden years. They are expected to be inactive, invisible, but happy. (p. 97)

An additional problem is that these expectations emphasize *proscriptions*, rules for what ought *not* to be done, rather than *prescriptions*, rules for what ought to be done. Thus, old people are not supposed to be interested in sex, should not marry, should not be creative, and should not be employed. Unfortunately, there are few expectations about what elders are supposed to do instead—except sit in their rocking chairs, reminisce, and prepare for death (Rosow, 1974). As a result, some elders become "imprisoned in a roleless role" (Burgess, 1960).

Faced with such ageism, elders respond in four basic ways: acceptance, denial, avoidance, or reform.

Acceptance. Just as among other minority groups, acceptance of the prejudice and discrimination against them may range from reluctant submission to complete endorsement. For example, Havighurst (1968) found a few elders who had voluntarily withdrawn from social and other activity, but remained satisfied with their lives. They were contented with their "rocking chair" position in life.

Another type of acceptance is found among the "apathetic." These elders have disengaged reluctantly and are not happy with their role. Both of these types have internalized elders stereotypes in the same way as they were socialized to accept other conceptions of appropriate behavior related to earlier life states. Throughout life there are subtle and sometimes overt sanctions to "act your age." In old age, these "age norms" tend to be more flexible and the sanctions are more informal, but they are nonetheless real and potent (Back, 1987).

Denial. This type of reaction is similar to the minority group reaction known as "passing." Some minority group members attempt to deny their negative status by passing for members of the dominant group: light skinned Blacks may pass for whites; Jews may change their name and pass for gentiles.

In a similar way, many aged refuse to identify themselves as old or aged, because of the negative connotations and stereotypes about old age (Drevenstedt, 1976). Taves and Hanson (1963) found only 5 percent of older residents of Minnesota thought of themselves as old at 65; more than 40 percent would not consider themselves as old until they were over 80.

Harris (1975) found that most people 65 and over expressed strong dislike for terms such as "old man" or "old woman," or even "aged person." They preferred to have themselves referred to as "senior citizen" or "mature American." As Bernard Baruch put it, "Old age is always 15 years older than I am."

There are no statistics on how many older men and women deny their age, but most authorities believe that many do and that lying about one's age is especially common among women. One article asserts, "The majority of women over 50 either feel guilty about their age—and confess to it as if admitting to the Brinks heist—or feel guilty about *lying* about their age" (Hodge, 1987, p. 40).

Denial of one's age is so common that it is usually considered impolite to even ask older persons how old they are. If, however, one does find out an older person's age, the polite response is, "You don't look that old." This remark is an encouragement of age denial, rather than pride in one's age. Furthermore, it is a dubious compliment, because it implies, "You don't look as feeble and senile as most people your age."

Age denial is a common source of jokes about elders. One of Jack Benny's most famous source of comedy was his assertion that he was only 39. A joke on a coffee mug says, "The secret of staying young is to find an age you *really like* and stick with it." This is an invitation to lie about one's age.

In my analysis of jokes about the elderly, I found that age denial is one of the most common themes, especially in jokes about old women (Palmore, 1971). This finding has since been replicated by several other studies (Palmore, 1986).

Some senior citizen clubs fine their members if they use the word "old." Before new business, the president calls for "leftover" business (not "old" business). It is as if being old is a disgrace (Jacobs & Vinick, 1977).

The attempts to pass for young or middle-aged provide major support for the multibillion dollar cosmetics industry, as well as the plastic surgery and false hair industries. Many advertisements for skin cream and hair dye promise or imply that their product can "make you look young again" and "prevent aging skin." Of course, cosmetics may be used simply to look attractive and healthy rather than to deny one's age.

The denial of "old" as a self-concept may actually be a denial of the negative age stereotypes, rather than a denial of chronological age. The denial that one is "old" may simply be an assertion that one still feels as healthy, strong, and vigorous as one did when younger. As Butler (1975, p. 14) points out, "the problem comes when this good feeling is called 'youth' rather than 'health', thus tying it to chronological age instead of to physical and mental well-being." This is another aspect of the semantic confusions between the concepts of aging and of deterioration (Chapter 6).

Levin and Levin (1980) assert, "Given the severe stigma of aging and the negative connotations associated with it, a middle-aged self-concept may actually sustain morale and increase satisfaction with life." There is considerable evidence that those elders who continue to consider themselves middle-aged are more healthy, more satisfied with life, and emotionally well adjusted than those who consider themselves "old" or "elderly" (Taves & Hanson, 1963; George, 1985).

However, the question remains whether a younger self-concept tends to sustain better mental health or whether a younger self-concept is an effect of better mental health and satisfaction. Probably the effects run in both directions, because of the strength of ageism in our culture.

If we could eliminate ageism, if we could separate chronological age from the connotations of sickness and senility, there would be no benefit from denying one's chronological age, and there would be no association between one's self-concept and one's health and happiness.

Avoidance. Elders may react to ageism by attempting to avoid it through age-segregation, isolation, alcoholism, drug addiction, mental illness, or suicide.

Age segregated retirement communities serve to separate elders from the prejudice and discrimination of younger people. Fear of victimization and violence is often given as a reason for moving to a retirement community (Jacobs, 1974). The slights and indignities often experienced by elders in their dealings with the young can be minimized in segregated communities, where most of one's neighbors and contacts are in the same status as oneself. One is not so constantly reminded of the differences in status and appearance between "them" and "us."

However, such segregation may contribute to the belief that elders are a separate and different kind of people from the rest of society, who should remain isolated and invisible. Such segregation is known to reinforce prejudice and discrimination against racial and ethnic minority group members. Especially when healthy and vigorous elders retreat to such segregated communities, their visibility as examples of normal aging is reduced.

Elders may isolate themselves from contact with younger people even though living in an age-integrated community. It has been found that about four percent of the elders in the United States, Great Britain, and Denmark are extremely isolated (Townsend, 1968). They avoid leaving their home as much as possible, they order food and supplies by telephone to be delivered, they order clothes and other things by mail order catalogue, they pay bills by mail, and so on. In this way they can avoid face-to-face contact with younger people as effectively as if they lived in an age-segregated community. This isolation avoids facing ageism from younger people.

However, such isolation is thought to be mentally and even physically unhealthy. There is considerable evidence that social isolation can contribute to mental and physical illness, especially in old age (Kahana, 1987), but the direction of causality is not clear: mental and physical illness can cause isolation as well as vice versa. Involuntary isolation caused by ageism and by attempts to avoid the insults of ageism may be especially dangerous to one's health.

Alcoholism can also be a way of avoiding ageism. When one is drunk, one need not face the prejudice and discrimination, the ostracism, the loss of role and status that often result from ageism.

There is no clear evidence that the prevalence of alcoholism increases with age, but there is considerable evidence that alcohol has greater effects on older than younger persons (Wood, 1987). Thus, if persons continue to consume the same amount of alcohol as they age, they will tend to become more drunk more often.

One reason that alcoholism is not more apparent among the elderly may be that they can remain drunk more of the time without interfering with their role obligations, since these obligations usually have been reduced. Also, older alcoholics may be more sheltered by family and friends than younger alcoholics (Blazer & Pennybacker, 1984).

Nevertheless, Mishara and Kastenbaum (1980) made an extensive review of the literature on aging and alcoholism and concluded that about 10 percent of the elderly are "problem drinkers"—defined as persons who have either physical symptoms or social difficulties arising from alcohol use, such as problems with family, neighbors, employers, or police. Many studies have found that heavy drinking is an important variable for many of the elderly being treated in mental health programs. For example, 53 percent of the men and 30 percent of the women over 60 examined in a Texas psychiatric screening agency were diagnosed as suffering from alcoholism (Gaitz & Baer, 1971).

Thus, alcoholism may be used as a way of avoiding ageism and other problems of old age.

Drug abuse is another way to escape from ageism. There are three types of drug abuse: illegal drug use, misuse of prescription drugs, and misuse of nonprescription (over-the-counter) drugs. Illegal drug use by elders is relatively rare compared to that of younger people, and is limited mainly to heroin, other opiates, and marijuana (Whittington, 1987).

The major problem among elders is the misuse of prescription drugs. The extent of such misuse is difficult to estimate because little adequate epidemiological research has been done on this problem. However, one study with a representative sample found about seven percent who were "inappropriate users" of prescription psychoactive medications (Inciardi, McBride, Russe, & Wells, 1978). Most of this misuse was overuse, and such overuse tends to lead to drug addiction. Little is known about misuse of nonprescription drugs. Some of this drug abuse is caused by physician or patient error. But some drug abuse may represent attempts to escape from the effects of ageism and other miseries of old age.

Mental illness may also be a kind of escape from ageism. If the problems of old age become unbearable, one can escape into a fantasy world of psychosis. This has been called "avoidance psychosis" (Payne, Gibson, & Pittard, 1969). Avoidance psychosis rarely results from conscious choice, but often results from unbearable mental conflict and pain. The symptoms of avoidance psychosis may be indistinguishable from those of organic dementia.

The prevalence of various dementias increases in old age (Reisberg, 1983; Terry & Katzman, 1983), but the prevalence of neurosis and schizophrenia decreases, so that the overall rate of mental impairment is actually lower in old age than at younger ages (Myers et al., 1984). There is no way to estimate how much of this mental impairment results from ageism, but certainly ageism contributes to the stresses that can produce mental illness.

Suicide is the ultimate escape from ageism. Suicide rates increase sharply with age among males in the United States and other industrialized countries; but not among women (Kastenbaum, 1987). It is not entirely clear why the suicide rate is higher for older men than women; but part of the explanation is that men are more successful at suicide because they use more violent means of killing themselves (guns, hanging, jumping off high places).

The typical profile of the older suicide victim is a man who is depressed, socially isolated, not married, downwardly mobile, residing in an urban area, and suffering from illness or disability (Osgood, 1984). It seems probable that much of this isolation, depression, and so on, is caused by ageism.

Reform. In contrast to denial and avoidance, the reform response recognizes the prejudice and discrimination of ageism and seeks to eliminate it. This response has not been as prevalent as the other three, but there are scattered signs that Western society may be entering a new era in which the struggle for "age rights" will occur on a large scale (Levin & Levin, 1980).

Rose (1969) was one of the first to recognize that elders subculture is partly a counterculture which emerges from attempts to combat ageism. Cryns and Monk (1972) found that elders who are dissatisfied with their lives and have poor filial relationships are especially likely to express negative attitudes toward the young and the dominant culture. Cutler (1973) found that elders who perceive that elders have low prestige tend to support organized political activity on behalf of elders. Neugarten (1970) suggests that attempts to reduce ageism may grow as elders become increasingly aware of ageism and increasingly educated, healthier, and affluent:

> As they become accustomed to the politics of confrontation they see around them, they may also become a more demanding group. There are signs that this is already so, with, for example, appeals to "senior power" (in some ways analogous to the appeal to "black power"), and with more frequent newspaper accounts of groups of older people picketing and protesting over such local issues as reduced bus fares or better housing projects. (p. 17)

Many organizations of elders engage in reform efforts to combat negative ageism. The largest of these is the American Association of Retired Persons (AARP), with over 30 million members, but there are several others with similar goals (see Chapter 14). However, it must be recognized that these organizations also tend to support positive ageism; i.e., special programs and benefits for elders only.

On the individual level, many elders quietly challenge the stereotypes and prejudice against them by engaging in activities that do not conform to these stereotypes: they continue to be athletic, healthy, romantic, clever, involved, beautiful, and handsome. Such challenge by personal example may be more effective in reducing ageism than all the political action of all the organized groups combined (see Chapter 12).

SUMMARY

There are several gains from both negative and positive ageism. The gains from employment discrimination include more jobs and promotions for younger workers, reduced wage costs, avoiding the embarrassment and difficulty of evaluating older workers, and forcing the less able to retire. The gains from negative ageism include repressing the fear of aging and death, avoiding society's responsibilities toward elders, avoiding the expenses of proper care, satisfying pathological impulses for revenge, and gains in prestige and self-esteem for younger people. Even elders may gain self-esteem by comparing themselves to the negative stereotypes of most aged.

The gains for elders from positive ageism include employment advantages, retirement benefits and other income transfers, tax breaks, legal and political advantages, exploitation of family members, and free medical care. Because of these gains, many elders and service providers oppose reductions in positive ageism.

The personal costs to elders of negative ageism include the avoidance of sexual relations, new ideas, productivity, effective activity, and social engagement, in order to conform to the negative stereotypes of ageism. This conformity, in turn, reduces self-esteem and personal abilities, and induces deterioration of physical and mental health. Denial of the realities of aging also has its costs.

The costs to younger persons may include loss of contact with reality, reduction of effective problem solving, feelings of guilt, moral ambivalence, tensions between ideals and practice, projection, and development of authoritarian personalities.

Economic costs of ageism probably total over $178 billion per year, including tax breaks, Social Security and Medicare for affluent elders, and the lost productivity from retired workers. In addition, there are the costs of the many other special programs for elders provided under other Federal, state, and local programs.

The social costs include isolation of elders caused by residential segregation, disengagement of groups from elders, unnecessary institutionalization, and other forms of discrimination. This isolation can be very costly in terms of mental and physical illness it may produce. The costs to younger people include the loss of the wisdom elders possess, the loss of knowledge of what aging and "the old days" were really like, and loss of emotional support from elders. National costs include the unrealistic policies that fail to solve basic national problems.

Responses of elders include acceptance, denial, avoidance, and reform. Acceptance includes the volutarily disengaged and the apathetic. Denial includes those who "pass" for younger persons, who use cosmetics and plastic surgery to try to "look younger," and who try to maintain a "young" self-concept and life-style. Avoidance may take the form of segregation, isolation, alcoholism, drug addiction, mental illness, or even suicide. Reform may take the form of a subculture of elders, political activity, organizational lobbying, public education, and individual challenges by elders who refuse to conform to the negative stereotypes about elders.

We now turn to a discussion of ageism in the various institutional areas of our society.

Part III
Institutional Patterns

8
The Economy

Policy makers and the elderly themselves generally agree that economic security in old age is one of the most important problems needing solution. Yet, as in other areas of knowledge, misconceptions abound. Most aged are not poor; they are not the group most seriously hurt by inflation; they have not been forced to retire.

Schultz, 1980

As whoopies (well-off older people), we are appalled that so many in our financial and age status are continually trying to gain more benefits from government at all levels, often at the expense of the younger generation.

Marotta and Marotta, 1989

EMPLOYMENT DISCRIMINATION

The most common type of economic discrimination against elders is discrimination in employment. This discrimination may take the form of refusal to hire or promote older workers, or forcing retirement at a fixed age regardless of the worker's ability to keep working.

Despite legislation against employment discrimination, many employers continue to discriminate, as shown by the awards of over $24 billion to over 5,000 individuals for age discrimination in employment (Atchley, 1988). Many more cases are settled out of court. Additional evidence of discrimination in hiring older workers are the facts that unemployed older workers stay unemployed much longer than younger workers, suffer a greater earnings loss in a subsequent job (if they can get one), and are more likely to give up looking for another job following a layoff (U.S. Senate Special Committee on Aging, 1988).

Such discrimination is often based on the stereotypes that older workers do not produce as much or as well as younger workers, that they cannot learn new skills, that they are more expensive to employ, or that they need jobs less than younger workers. Rosen and Jerdee (1976a) found that managers stereotyped older workers as resistant to change, uncreative, cautious and slow to make judgments, lower in physical capacity, uninterested in technological change, and untrainable.

To find out how these stereotypes influence managerial decisions Rosen and Jerdee (1976b) presented a group of 42 business students in their twenties with an "in-basket" exercise involving six memos requiring action by a manager. To discover the effect of age, they referred to the focal person in the memo either as "younger" or "older"; in addition, four cases included a personnel file with a photograph of a younger or older person enclosed. Since each participant received only one version of the six cases, the manipulation of the age variable was unobtrusive.

From the results, Rosen and Jerdee concluded that the business students' assumptions about the physical, mental, and emotional characteristics of older workers produced managerial decisions that were contrary to the well-being and career progress of older employees. Decisions about hiring, retention, correction, training, and retraining all suffered purely because of the age of the employee.

In a similar study, graduate business students indicated they would be much less likely to hire 60- and 70-year-old applicants than they would 35- and 50-year-old applicants who were identical in every way except their age (Craft, Doctors, Shkop, & Benecki, 1979).

Surveys have found that 80 percent of adults believe that most employers discriminate against older workers, and 61 percent of employers agreed that they do (U.S. Senate Special Committee on Aging, 1988).

Such discrimination ignores the several advantages of employing older workers: older workers tend to have less absenteeism, less accidents, less turnover, less alcoholism and drug addiction; but more job satisfaction and company loyalty (Krauss, 1987; Doering, Rhodes, & Schuster, 1983).

LEGISLATION ON EMPLOYMENT DISCRIMINATION

In order to reduce such discrimination, the Age Discrimination in Employment Act (ADEA) was enacted in 1967 and amended in 1974, 1978, and 1986. The ADEA now prohibits mandatory retirement based on age for most federal, state, and private employees. It currently allows firefighters, police, and tenured college faculty to be exempt from its provisions, but these exemptions will be terminated in 1993.

However, mandatory retirement based on age will still be allowed even after 1993 for elected public officials and their staff, and highly paid executives with annual retirement benefits of at least $44,000. The apparent rationale is that it is difficult to fairly and accurately evaluate competence in such high level positions.

In addition, certain other occupations are exempt from the ADEA if the employer can prove that age is a "bona fide occupational qualification." Airplane pilots are the main occupation affected by this exemption. The Federal Aviation Administration (FAA) currently prohibits employment of persons over age 60 from flying commercial jet airplanes.

However, this FAA ruling is being challenged on the grounds that the research on which it is based is inadequate to justify the rule and because two pilots who recently have shown outstanding ability by their performance in potential airplane disasters were age 59 at the time (and were forced to retire one year later) (Stephens, 1989).

The ADEA legislation has made it possible for many competent workers to continue employment past the traditional retirement age, but it has not reversed the long-term trend toward more and earlier retirement. By 1986 only 16 percent of men and 7 percent of women over 65 were in the labor force (U.S. Senate Special Committee on Aging, 1986). Thus, fears that this legislation would flood the labor market with elders were unjustified. The increasing availability of comfortable pensions and other incentives to retire have made fewer older workers willing to continue working.

Some experts in the field say that as a result of such legislation, older workers sometimes have an advantage over younger workers, because employers fear lawsuits against them based on allegations of age discrimination (Attorney Normam Smith, personal communication). This is a good example of how negative ageism may be reversed to become positive ageism.

In their attempts to avoid charges of age discrimination, some employers are deliberately trying to hire older workers. Some Help Wanted advertisements now specify that applicants must be "55 years or older." This is really another kind of age discrimination, but discrimination in *favor* of older workers.

POSITIVE DISCRIMINATION IN EMPLOYMENT

There are a few jobs in our society for which older age appears to be an advantage: judges, senators, governors, ambassadors, presidents of colleges and corporation boards, and other such high level occupations. However, it could be argued that this is not discrimination in favor of older people, but discrimination in favor of experience and the wisdom that can develop from years of experience. But since such experience requires older age, the distinction between experience and age becomes a moot point.

There are several federally funded employment programs for low-income older workers. The largest of these is the Senior Community Service Employment Program established by the Older Americans Act (Title V), which provides part-time public service employment at the minimum wage for people 55 and older who have incomes no higher than 125 percent of the federal poverty level. This employment provides aides to schools, libraries, hospitals, and social service agencies. In 1983 $282 million was spent on this program.

Another such program is the Foster Grandparent Program, which employs low-income elders to help children in schools, homes for retarded or disturbed children, homes for infants, care centers, and convalescent hospitals. Their goal is to provide a person-to-person relationship with individual children and to supply an affectionate concern for the child, which is often missing in such institutions. In addition to their stipend, foster grandparents receive a daily hot meal, transportation allowance, and an annual physical examination. In 1981, 18,000 volunteers were employed, serving some 54,000 children (Peterson, 1987).

The Green Thumb Program is similar to the Foster Grandparent Program, except that the Green Thumb workers are from rural areas and work at beautifying parks and roadsides or serve as aides in schools and libraries. There are also numerous local programs providing special employment opportunities for elders.

Such programs undoubtedly contribute to the good health and spirits of thousands of elders and children, as well as to the financial health of the older workers. However, they can be criticized on two grounds. First, it has been argued that there are not enough such positions to meet the great demand for them. Only 1 percent of elders are employed in any such program, while it is estimated that at least 20 percent need such employment (Peterson, 1987).

On the other hand, such programs show positive ageism in that they exclude younger people from participation. According to this criticism, the programs should be opened to low-income people of all ages.

INCOME AND ASSETS

Retirement income is usually lower than preretirement income in the United States (although not in Scandinavian countries), because the combination of pension and Social Security benefits is typically less than preretirement earnings (Clark, 1987). For example, the average family income of a household with a head 65 or older is about half that of households whose head is 45 to 54.

However, part of this difference is due to cohort (generational) differences: today's elders have never been as affluent as today's younger generation. When one controls for preretirement characteristics and the effects of aging, the average retiree retains about three-fourths of preretirement income (Palmore, Burchett, Fillenbaum, George, & Wallman, 1985).

Furthermore, family cash income is not a good measure of the relative economic status of elders, for several reasons. First, older households tend to be smaller because there are no children in them. Several studies have concluded that the per capita income of older families is the same as or higher than the per capita income of younger families (Clark, 1987).

Second, elders receive substantial in-kind transfers of goods and services from the government and private agencies. Chief among these are medical services through Medicare and Medicaid, subsidized housing, subsidized food, and home energy assistance. These benefits have an annual cash value of over $3,000 for the average elderly couple (Smeeding, 1982).

One could argue that such benefits are partially offset by increased needs for medical and other care among elders. But one could also argue that these increased needs are balanced by *decreased* needs for education of children, clothing, life insurance, savings for retirement, and so on.

Third, elders tend to have more assets (wealth) than younger persons. The median net worth of households with a head 65 and over was $60,266 in 1984 compared to a median net worth for all households of $32,677 (U.S. Senate Special Committee on Aging, 1988).

Another indication of the relative affluence of elders is that poverty rates among those 65 and over have fallen below those of the rest of the population (U.S. Senate Special Committee on Aging, 1986). While certain subgroups, such as older Black women and widowed women, continue to have high rates of poverty, this is partly because of their race, sex, and marital status.

Certainly, the stereotype that elders as a group tend to be poor is no longer true. Thus this stereotype can no longer be used to justify special programs and benefits for elders as a group. In fact, it can be agued that elders are now *less* needy than any other age group.

INFLATION

Many assume that the income of elders tends to be more fixed than the income of younger people, and that elders are therefore especially vulnerable to inflation. This belief is used to justify special income supports, tax breaks, and other special benefits for elders.

Recent research has found that this belief is no longer true (if it ever was true). Social Security benefits are now fully indexed to the rate of inflation, and other forms of government income supports are implicitly or explicitly indexed to changes in consumer prices (i.e., the income increases as much as prices increase). Many employer pensions tend to grant increases to keep up with inflation. The earnings of those still employed also tend to go up with inflation. Thus, few elders live on truly fixed incomes. Available data indicate that for elders, both real income and income relative to that of younger people rose during the high inflation years of the 1970s (Clark, Maddox, Schrimper, & Sumner, 1984).

In other words, elders were hurt by inflation *less* than younger people. Therefore, special benefits for elders can no longer be justified by the assumption that they are specially vulnerable to inflation.

SOCIAL SECURITY

Almost all elders are eligible for Social Security benefits or an equivalent government pension. The main groups not covered are

low paid and short-term workers in farm and domestic employment. Nine out of 10 people 65 or older receive some income from
Social Security, and one-third depend on Social Security for 80
percent or more of their income (U.S. Senate Special Committee
on Aging, 1988).

The total Social Security and veterans compensation benefits
amounted to $182 billion in 1986. This was about 18 percent of
total federal outlays and was the largest single item in the budget
(U.S. Senate Special Committee on Aging, 1988). When all forms of
federal outlays for elders are added together, they amount to one-
third of total federal expenditures (Laurie, 1987).

It can be argued that this massive program is a form of positive
ageism because one must be aged to receive these retirement benefits.
The counterargument is that Social Security retirement benefits and
government pensions are meant to be a reward for a lifetime of work
and of contributions to the Social Security system; and that age is
just an indirect measure for these years of contributions.

If this argument is valid, it would seem that changing the
eligibility criteria from years of age to years of contribution would
eliminate the charge of ageism and still meet the goal of reserving
benefits for those who have completed a normal lifetime of work.

SUPPLEMENTAL SECURITY INCOME (SSI)

This is a joint federal-state program of public assistance to needy
older people. It is, in effect, a guaranteed annual income for persons over 65 (as well as for blind and disabled younger persons). In
1987 it guaranteed an income of $510 per month for couples and
$340 for individuals. Approximately 1.5 million people were en-
rolled in the program, and it is estimated that another 1.5 million
would have been eligible if they had applied for it (U.S. Senate
Special Committee on Aging, 1985). This program cost $3.7 billion
in 1986.

SSI can also be criticized as ageist since one must be aged to
qualify (unless blind or disabled). The obvious answer to this
criticism is to make low-income persons of all ages eligible. This
would, of course, increase the costs by perhaps 10 times (from $3
billion to $30 billion), but this cost would be largely offset by
eliminating the need for most other welfare programs. A more
modest change would be to change the eligibility criteria from an
age requirement to one of years of service (including child rearing,
housekeeping, and so on).

TAXATION

Elders enjoy several tax breaks (technically called "tax expenditure") that are not available to younger persons. The largest of these is the exclusion of Social Security and Railroad Retirement benefits from the federal income tax. This tax break cost the government over $13 billion in 1985 (Hudson, 1987).

In 1987 this tax break was modified so that individuals with over $32,000 (not counting Social Security benefits) have to pay tax on one-half of their Social Security benefits. However, this new provision recaptures only a small proportion of the cost of this tax break.

Another large tax break for elders is the exclusion of capital gains on home sales for people 55 and over. This cost the government almost $1 billion in 1985 (Hudson, 1987).

Prior to 1987, people over 65 were allowed a double personal exemption on the federal income tax. This cost the government $2.5 billion in 1985 (Hudson, 1987). In 1987 this was modified so that there is an additional exemption of $750 for an individual and $1,200 for a couple over 65 for those who use the standard deduction.

A relatively small tax break is the tax credit for low income elders (and disabled). This cost the government $200 million in 1985 (Hudson, 1987).

In addition to these federal tax breaks, most state and local governments provide various income and property tax breaks for elders. For example, North Carolina allows an extra personal exemption of $1,100 for each individual over 65. There has been no estimate of how many billions of dollars these tax breaks cost state and local governments.

A major criticism of such tax breaks is that they tend to favor higher income elders more than lower income elders, thus widening the gap between affluent and poor elders (Nelson, 1983). Others argue that elders deserve or need such tax breaks. But regardless of these arguments, all such tax breaks are, by definition, ageist because they are available only to elders. Whatever the justification in the past, it seems no longer equitable to give affluent elders tax breaks just because they are over 65, while denying such breaks to younger persons who may need them more.

SUMMARY

Many employers continue to discriminate against elders despite recent legislation against such discrimination. This discrimination is based on stereotypes that older workers do not produce as much or as well as younger workers, that older workers cannot learn new skills, that it is cheaper to employ younger workers, or that younger workers need jobs more than older workers. Such ageism ignores the many advantages of employing older workers.

On the other hand, there is some positive discrimination in favor of elders for some jobs such as judges, senators, and other such high level occupations. There are also several state and local employment programs restricted to older workers. Regardless of the merits of such programs they are clearly ageist, because they are not available to younger workers.

Special programs and benefits to elders can no longer be justified by the assumption that elders tend to be poorer or that they are more vulnerable to inflation. This is largely due to improvements in the Social Security and Supplemental Security Income programs, as well as to better pensions and increased assets among elders. Nevertheless, the Social Security and SSI programs are ageist in that they are limited to older persons.

Special tax breaks for elders are another large and costly set of ageist policies. Alternatives to such age discrimination would be to extend such benefits to all ages, or to use years of service rather than age as the criteria for eligibility.

9

The Government

The government provides benefits and services to the elderly in a fragmented, inefficient, unmanageable, and incomprehensible way.
Congressman Claude Pepper, 1979

Those who allege that old age is devoid of useful activity adduce nothing to the purpose, and are like those who would say that the pilot does nothing in the sailing of the ship, because, while others are climbing the masts, or running about the gangways, or working the pumps, he sits quietly in the stern and simply holds the tiller which steers the ship. He may not be doing what the younger members of the crew are doing, but what he does is better and much more important. It is not by muscle, speed, or physical dexterity that great things are achieved, but by reflection, force of character, and judgement; in these qualities old age is not only not poorer, but is even richer.
Cicero, quoted in McKee, 1982

POSITIVE AGEISM IN GOVERNMENT PROGRAMS

Most of the numerous government programs for elders are described in detail in other chapters. Here we will only list the major programs and indicate how big they are (Oriol, 1987; U.S. Senate Special Committee on Aging, 1988). All of these programs represent positive ageism. Ironically, these positive programs are usually based on *negative* stereotypes held by legislators: the elderly are inadequate workers, are in poor health, are in poverty, are isolated, are old-fashioned, and are mentally slow (Lubomudrov, 1987).

- Old Age and Survivors Insurance (Social Security) paid 22 million retired beneficiaries and 3.5 million of their dependents in 1984. It cost $146 billion in 1986.
- Supplemental Security Income (SSI) made payments to 2 million persons 65 and over, which cost $3.7 billion in 1986.
- Civil Service Retirement in 1985 paid benefits to 1.3 million retired.
- Military Retirement in 1985 paid $15 billion in pensions.
- Railroad Retirement System in 1985 paid $6 billion into their trust fund for retirees.
- Medicare in 1987 had about 28 million aged eligible for benefits and paid out $70 billion.
- Area Agencies on Aging (AAA) in 1985 had over 660 AAAs, 8,000 service providers, 78,000 volunteers, and 230,000 meal program volunteers.
- Public Housing in 1986 had about 500,000 housing units for elders. Another 168,000 elders and their families received subsidized housing through Section 202, which provides loans to private nonprofit sponsors. About $4.9 billion was spent on such subsidized housing.
- Senior Community Service Employment in 1986 cost $323 million.
- Other employment programs for elders include Foster Grandparents, Green Thumb, Retired Seniors, and Senior Home Aides. These cost about $106 million in 1986.
- National Institute on Aging (NIA) in 1985 cost $150 million.
- Federal Council on Aging is responsible for overseeing all executive branch activities affecting older persons.

In addition to these federal programs, state governments are becoming increasingly important in developing and supporting special programs for elders (Lammers, 1987). The most expensive state income support programs are the state retirement systems. In 1982 state governments paid out over $12 billion in benefits to their retirees. The largest direct expenditures involve geriatric health care, primarily through Medicaid. In addition, many states also contribute substantial sums to supplement SSI payments.

Local governments also provide numerous programs for elders through direct service, supplements to federal and state programs, and tax reductions.

It should be clear that major portions of our federal, state, and local governments are devoted to special programs for elders, which represent positive ageism because younger people are not eligible to participate in them. Chapter 13 discusses whether such programs are desirable and how they might be modified to make them nonageist.

NEGATIVE AGEISM IN GOVERNMENT PROGRAMS

Despite the generally positive form of most ageism in government programs, there is considerable evidence that the way some federal programs are administered produces discrimination against elders. The U.S. Commission on Civil Rights (1977) found that several federally funded programs often discriminate against elders, in such areas as: community mental health centers, legal services, vocational rehabilitation, social services to low-income persons, employment and training services, the Food Stamp program, Medicaid, and vocational education. They also found that such discrimination was most prevalent against the older elderly.

The Commission concluded that much of this discrimination stems from narrow interpretations of the goals of the legislation that established the program. For example, community health centers generally interpreted "preventive health care" as applying only to children and adolescents, when in fact older people need such care as much as younger people. For other examples, employment programs concentrate their efforts on males ages 22 to 44; and job training programs are often reserved for those under 25.

The Commission also concluded that state legislatures sometimes convert federal programs designed to serve all ages into categorical programs for special age groups. For example, the state of Missouri earmarked for child abuse programs most of the funds that were allocated by the federal government for general social services to all ages. As a result most cities in the state discontinued their protective services programs for other age groups.

Several states exclude older people from vocational rehabilitation programs on the assumption that they are not "of employable age." This is a recognition of the fact that both public and private job markets tend to discriminate against elders in their hiring practices.

Several gerontologists have recently criticized ageism in government programs. Crystal (1982) asserted that federal age-specific programs have resulted in "two worlds of aging" in which the "better off" are served disproportionately, while the "worse off" are neglected. Binstock (1983) asserted that "compassionate ageism" directs assistance where it may not be needed while neglecting fundamental needs. Neugarten (1983) pointed out that age-specific programs tend to perpetuate stereotypical images of all old persons as dependent and at risk, making it more difficult to target those actually in need of help.

A controversial example of discrimination against elders are the driver's license testing requirements, which are different from those for everyone else. Several states now have such discriminatory requirements. They are justified by the fact that older drivers have a higher rate of accidents-per-mile than middle-aged drivers (see Chapter 2). But drivers under age 25 have the highest rate of all and no special testing requirement exists for them.

POLITICS

In this area there appears to be both positive ageism and negative ageism. The positive ageism is seen in the fact that holders of political office tend to be older men (and some older women). This is especially true of the higher officials such as mayors, judges, senators, governors, and Presidents. In fact, this tendency is found throughout history and across all types of political systems (Hudson & Strate, 1985).

However, a question may be raised as to whether this tendency is due to prejudice in favor of older people or to the greater experience that older age usually confers. It may be that the greater advantage of older men in politics is mainly due to the time and experience needed to build up the power base necessary to get into public office. Most people probably recognize that while years of experience do not necessarily bring wisdom in public affairs, years of experience are a prerequisite for mature wisdom.

Turner and Kahn (1974) found that age of a candidate was an insignificant issue among voters of all ages. However, experience *was* a salient factor. Furthermore, Schlesinger and Schlesinger (1981) concluded that "American politics has not been especially cordial to the older political neophyte" (p. 235).

The political power of elders as a voting bloc could be cited as another kind of positive ageism. It appears that no major politician dares to oppose the basic income provisions of Social Security. There is widespread concern in politics about the "old folks vote."

However, the belief that elders form a unified interest group that can mobilize political pressure by bloc voting is an illusion and is likely to remain so (Binstock, 1972). The passage of pro-aged legislation and the continuing support for these programs is due less to the power of elders than it is to the power of the younger relatives and friends in various organizations such as unions, professional associations, and political parties, who support these programs.

Such support from younger people is based on a mixture of altruism and self-interest: they are sympathetic to the plight of needy aged, but they are also aware that if the government does not provide income support and pay for health care of elders, younger relatives would usually have to do so. Furthermore, most younger persons are aware that they too will probably become old someday and therefore will benefit from programs for elders.

In addition to such positive ageism, there are occasional signs of negative ageism in politics. Older candidates for office are sometimes characterized as being "old-fashioned," "senile," or "worn out." Of course, such charges may be true and not the result of ageism.

CRIME

One of the most striking differences between younger and older people is the low rate of criminal acts by elders. The aged are the most law-abiding of all age groups, regardless of how criminality is measured. For example, persons over 65 have about one-tenth the arrest rate for all offenses that others have, and about one twentieth the arrest rate for felony offenses (Federal Bureau of Investigation, 1981). Similarly, persons 65 and over are incarcerated in prisons and jails at about one-tenth the overall rate (U.S. Bureau of the Census, 1981).

Elders are more law-abiding than younger people for a number of reasons: criminals tend to either die young or "retire" from crime before they reach old age; elders usually have more assets and economic security than most adolescents and young adults; elders may have learned from experience that "crime does not pay."

But the question has been raised as to whether some of this difference in crime rates may be due to positive ageism on the part of police, attorneys, juries, and judges. There is some evidence that behavior treated as criminal in younger people may be viewed as less serious when committed by older people. For example, Stephens (1976) reports a case of an elderly woman who engaged in indecent exposure, but was ignored by the residents of her hotel because of her age. For another example, Frankfather (1977) reported that police would ignore all sorts of strange behavior by the elderly because they perceive it as harmless and due to senility.

In addition, positive ageism may show itself in a tendency for attorneys to use more plea bargaining for older offenders, for juries to convict older defendants less often, and for judges to give more lenient sentences and more parole, especially when the older person has a relatively "clean" record or appears to have few years left to live. There is no solid evidence as to how often such discrimination in favor of older offenders occurs, but it could easily result from the stereotype of elders as being kind, honest, and trustworthy.

Chaneles (1987), a criminologist, asserts:

> I believe the facts [about criminality among elders] are obscured by a double standard of law enforcement toward older men and women. Except for the most serious crimes, such as murder, police and prosecutors are inclined to overlook offenses by the elderly, especially women. They often don't make arrests, or if they do, the charges are dismissed. (p. 49)

CRIMINAL VICTIMIZATION

This is another area in which one might suspect ageism because many believe that elders are more often victims of crime. This belief is based on the stereotype of the weak and vulnerable old person. On the contrary, elders are *less* often victimized in almost all categories of crime (Cutler, 1987). Only in the category of larceny with personal contact (e.g., purse snatching) is the rate higher for older than for younger persons; and even here there is little difference.

There are a number of explanations for these low rates of criminal victimization. The aged are more fearful of crime and therefore are more cautious and avoid dangerous situations and areas. Elders tend to stay home more and therefore discourage burglary and theft. Elders are less likely to provoke violent crimes by aggressive behavior.

However, ageism may also play a role: negative stereotypes such as the belief that elders are poor and have little worth stealing may make them less attractive targets for property crimes. It seems unlikely that positive ageism in the form of empathy or affection for elders would reduce the amount of crime against them.

There is evidence that elders are more vulnerable to one type of crime: fraud and medical quackery (U.S. Senate Special Committee on Aging, 1965). Frequent types of fraud against elders involve the sale of worthless property (for a "retirement home"), confidence games, fraudulent "pre-need" funeral payment plans, worthless "medical devices" and "cures." Such crimes against elders are probably encouraged by the stereotype that older people tend to be more gullible, ignorant about medical science, and desperate to try any possible cure for their disease. This stereotype is probably more true of aged than of younger people; ageism is involved when criminals pick elders as their victims because the criminals think most aged fit this stereotype.

SUMMARY

Positive ageism is reflected in the many and massive government programs for elders such as Social Security and Medicare, because they serve only elders (and their dependents). However, negative ageism is reflected in the way some government programs are administered, such as community mental health centers, vocational rehabilitation, employment, and training services. These programs tend to discriminate against older persons because of the way they define their primary clientele.

Several gerontologists have pointed out that age-specific government programs tend to provide services where they are not needed and to neglect services to those who do need them.

Positive ageism may be reflected in the tendency for office-holders to be older people, although this is probably because of their greater experience, rather than their older age as such. The success of legislation and programs for elders is less a result of the power of "the old folks vote" and more the result of a broad coalition of all ages reflecting self-interest as well as sympathy for the needy aged.

Part of the explanation for the apparent rarity of criminality among elders may be that law enforcement officials tend to be more lenient with older offenders. The low rate of criminal victimization (for most types of crime) may be partly explained by the stereotypes that elders are less likely to have much worth stealing. Elders are probably more victimized by fraud and medical quackery, partly because of the stereotype that elders tend to be more gullible and desperate for any possible cures for their diseases.

10
The Family

*When hair is snow-white,
what can warm the heart? Only
family and friends.*
                    Japanese Haiku (Palmore & Maeda, 1985)

Less than five percent of the older population are without family.
                                              Atchley, 1988

MARRIAGE AND REMARRIAGE

Most elders (95%) are or have been married (U.S. Bureau of the Census, 1984a). This is true of both older men and women. However, when older men become widowed or divorced they are most likely to remarry, while older women are more likely to remain widowed or divorced. This is reflected in several statistics: there are over five times as many widows as widowers among elders, yet twice as many widowers as widows remarry each year (Schick, 1986); and about three-fourths of women over 75 are widowed or divorced, but only one-quarter of men over 75 (U.S. Bureau of the Census, 1984a).

Part of the explanation for this difference in remarriage rates between men and women is demographic: older women outnumber older men by three to two. Thus, even if the rates of widowhood and divorce were equal between older men and women, and they remarried only persons their own age, there would still not be enough men for one-third of the women.

124

Another important explanation involves a gender-specific form of ageism: few men marry women older than themselves, but many men marry women younger than themselves (National Center for Health Statistics, 1984). This is true of both first and later marriages. Apparently, men of all ages tend to view women who are older than themselves as less attractive potential mates than women their own age or younger. Similarly, women tend to prefer men older than themselves. Therefore, older women find it very difficult to remarry, both because of the shortage of unmarried men their age or older, and because of the discrimination against them by men of all ages.

In addition, there is evidence that widowed women are often less motivated to remarry than men: in comparison to men, widowed women get more social support, have less difficulty keeping busy, and are more able to take care of themselves (Vinick, 1979).

Ageism tends to depress remarriage rates in general because of the widespread assumption that elders are, or should be, sexless and therefore do not need to remarry:

> Apparently, considerable social pressure is exerted against marriage in later life, probably growing partly out of a misguided notion that older people do not *need* to be married and partly out of concern over what will happen to their estates. Older people are very sensitive to this pressure, and encouragement from children and from friends is important in overcoming it. (Atchley, 1988, p. 142)

This opposition to remarriage is indeed misguided. In addition to continuing sexual need, older people have continuing needs for emotional intimacy, companionship, interdependency, caring, and a sense of belonging, all of which can usually be best satisfied through marriage.

SEXUAL INTIMACY

One of the most common and cruel myths about aging is that most elders have no interest in nor capacity for sexual activity. This myth appears to have its roots in the teachings of the medieval church that sexual activity among older people is "unnatural" and immoral (Covey, 1989).

On the contrary, the majority of persons past age 65 continue to have both interest in and capacity for sexual activity. Masters and

Johnson (1966) found that the capacity for satisfying sexual relations usually continues into the decades of the seventies and eighties for healthy couples. The Duke Longitudinal Studies (Palmore,
1981) also found that sex continues to play an important role in the
lives of the majority of men and women through the seventh
decade of life. A survey of elders (Starr & Weiner, 1981) found that
most indicated their sexual activity after 60 was as satisfying or
more satisfying than when younger.

Prejudice against sexuality in late life has several unhealthy effects.
It may prevent elders from seeking satisfying sexual relations because
they think it is "normal" to ignore their sexuality. It may discourage
them from seeking a new sexual partner after they have become
widowed or divorced. Even the sexually active elders may feel guilty
about their sexuality and hide it for fear of disapproval.

A recent analysis of 65 advice books for elders found that sexual
activity is encouraged more now than in the past, but that there is
still little support for dating and remarriage (Arluke, Levine, &
Suchwalko, 1984).

ELDER ABUSE AND NEGLECT

This topic has received widespread and often sensational attention
by the media in recent years. As a result, 37 states (as of 1986) had
laws mandating that elder abuse and neglect be reported to government agencies (Thobaden & Anderson, 1985). An official estimate is that four percent of all older people are abused each year
(U.S. House Select Committee on Aging, 1981).

However, actual physical abuse, such as hitting, slapping, or
using physical restraints, is the least common form of abuse. Much
more common are passive neglect, verbal or emotional abuse, and
financial exploitation (Hickey & Douglass, 1981). It seems debatable whether *neglect* should be called "abuse" at all.

The actual extent and incidence of abuse, by any definition, is
unknown (Pedrick-Cornell & Gelles, 1982), but physical abuse is
probably rare, involving less than one percent of elders.

Furthermore, most elder abuse and neglect is not due to ageism,
but to attempts at exploitation, or escape from care-giving duties,
or resentment at being dependent, or revenge for being abused as a
child, or to some form of mental illness (Quinn, 1987a). However,
elder abuse and neglect are encouraged by the stereotypes of the

old as helpless, worthless, and repulsive. These stereotypes encourage people to vent their frustrations on elders or to see them as vulnerable targets for exploitation.

ABUSE OF YOUNGER RELATIVES

The reverse of elder abuse is abuse of offspring. Elders may physically abuse, emotionally abuse, or neglect their adult children or grandchildren who are dependent on them for care and support. However, there have been few reports of such problems and no research on this topic. Furthermore, it seems unlikely that this would be due to ageism, but most likely due to the same motivations that cause elder abuse (see preceding paragraph).

A more frequent phenomenon is exploitation of adult children based on the principle of filial responsibility. About half of the states have laws that require children of "any person in need who is unable to maintain themself by work, to maintain such person to the extent of their ability" (Borgatta, 1987, p. 256).

It is probable that some older parents take advantage of such laws or of their children's sense of duty, and demand more support and care than they need. This could be a form of ageism if it were based on stereotypes of older persons as being helpless and needy.

However, there has been little published research in this area and we have no information as to the extent of such exploitation (Schorr, 1961).

SUMMARY

Remarriage rates are much higher among older men than women, largely because of a gender-specific form of ageism: few men want to marry older women. Remarriage among older persons is often discouraged by the misguided assumption that elders are or should be sexless. The myth of asexuality among elders can also be responsible for sexual deprivation and feelings of guilt and shame.

Most elder abuse is not motivated by ageism, but negative stereotypes may encourage it. The reverse of elder abuse is abuse of younger relatives by elders, but we have no information on the extent of such abuse. Exploitation of one's children may be related to stereotypes that the aged tend to be helpless and needy.

11

Housing and Health Care

Housing is more than a place to live.

Atchley, 1986

As the twentieth century draws to a close, the organization, financing, and use of health care in the United States is undergoing continuous and major revisions.

Binstock, 1987

RESIDENTIAL SEGREGATION

Because housing is more than a place to live, it can have many functions: a symbol of independence, a focal point for family gatherings; a source of pleasant memories; a link to the community; a focus of useful activities such as hobbies and crafts, gardening, and home improvement. Because of these many functions, age-segregation in housing can have major consequences.

Age-segregated housing ranges from retirement communities and buildings that do not allow any residents under a certain age, to neighborhoods and buildings where elders are concentrated because there are special attractions for them. Among the attractions may be a lower crime rate; less noise from children; easy access to public transportation, health care, and other facilities; special programs for elders; and older neighbors with similar interests and life-style to their own. Also segregated communities may be preferred in order to avoid the daily slights and feelings of

128

inferiority that may result from living in age-integrated communities (see Chapter 7).

However, there are several possible costs to such segregation. The elders may feel isolated and cut off from the rest of society. They may miss the normal interaction with persons of all ages. They may develop feelings of neglect and hostility toward younger people because of their isolation.

Costs to younger people include deprivation from normal interaction and affection from older people, the loss of knowledge about what old age is really like, the reinforcement of stereotypes, and the loss of elders' services such as baby-sitting, home repairs, and so on. In general, age segregation probably encourages more ageism, just as racial segregation encourages racism.

One subtle form of ageism is community opposition to in-migration of elders. This has been described as the "gray peril mentality":

> There is an impression in some parts of the South that retirement migration is Grant's revenge. One senses the low-grade anxiety in statements decrying the burden placed on local social services by all those poor old people moving down from up North. There is more than a hint of Southern localism in this sentiment and perhaps an undertone of xenophobia as well; after all, if all those old Yankees move down here, there won't be enough help to go around for our own old folks at home. One is reminded of Oriental immigration in California nearly a century ago that came to be called the yellow peril. This *gray* peril mentality, however, has been very difficult to document. (Longino, 1988, p. 448)

SUBSIDIZED HOUSING

In addition to regular public housing for which low-income elders are eligible, there is the Section 202 Housing for the Elderly and Handicapped Program, which provides low-interest loans for housing projects for low-income elderly and the handicapped. Since the program's authorization in 1959, over 168,000 units have been constructed as of 1985 (U.S. Senate Special Committee on Aging, 1985).

Elders are also eligible for the Congregate Housing Service Program, which awards grants to public housing authorities and the nonprofit sponsors of section 202 projects to provide meals and supportive services to partially impaired elderly and handicapped persons. The objective of the program, which served more than

2,700 elderly in 1984, is to enable the frail elderly to remain in their own dwellings and to avoid unnecessary institutionalization. State and local governments also have numerous housing programs for elders only.

These federal, state, and local programs are examples of positive ageism, because they provide benefits to elders for which younger people are not eligible. One might argue that younger people are eligible for other housing programs. But elders have the advantage of being eligible for both the regular programs for all ages and the special programs for elders only. As a result, elders are overrepresented in public housing: in 1984 almost half (46%) of all public housing units were occupied by persons 65 and over (U.S. Senate Special Committee on Aging, 1985). This is ageism.

One argument for special housing for elders is that elders tend to need special facilities, such as grab bars, handrails, wheel chair access, and congregate nutrition centers. The answer to this argument is that healthy older people do not need these facilities any more than younger people do. If serving the handicapped is the goal, then the housing could be designated as housing for the handicapped, rather than for the elderly. This would eliminate the ageism.

Another argument for special housing for elders is that many elders prefer to live in age-segregated housing without children and youth, because of the commotion and crime the younger persons cause. But if this were the goal, it would be possible to restrict the project to adults, as do many private housing developments. This would not eliminate all of the ageism, but at least it would not discriminate against childless younger adults.

If older people prefer to live in age-segregated housing *and* can afford to pay for it themselves, they have a right to do so. However, it is debatable whether the government should use public funds to pay for housing programs that discriminate against younger persons.

ARCHITECTURE

Architecture specifically designed for older adults has become big business and has developed a new specialty within the profession of architecture (Gelwicks, 1987). It began in the late 1940s in response to the demand for an increasing number of homes for elders and nursing homes. It grew rapidly throughout the 1950s and 1960s through the encouragement of major governmental agencies such as the Federal Housing Administration, Public Housing Administration, the Administration on Aging, and the Department of Housing and Urban Development.

Private organizations such as the National Council on the Aging and the American Association of Retired Persons also supported research, training, and demonstration projects for improving the design of housing for the elderly. Many books have been published in the field, such as *Buildings for the Elderly* (Musson & Heusink-veld, 1963) and *Planning Housing Environments for the Elderly* (Gelwicks & Newcomer, 1974; see also Lawton, 1980).

However, when one examines this literature, one finds that it does not really deal with architecture for elders in general, but with architecture for the frail and handicapped. Since the majority of elders are neither frail nor handicapped, the majority do not need any specially designed housing.

Why then does this field refer to itself as architecture "for the elderly" rather than "for the handicapped"? Perhaps it uses "elderly" as a euphemism for handicapped because many older people might not want to admit that they are handicapped. Or perhaps it is another example of the confusion between "old" and "impaired." In any case, equating "elderly" with "handicapped" perpetuates the negative stereotypes of ageism.

Such concerns may appear to be mere semantic quibbles. However, it is such semantic confusion that tends to reinforce ageism and its stereotypes. When an architect proclaims that a given building was designed for the elderly and then shows that its major features are designed to accommodate people with handicaps, that architect is reinforcing the stereotype that most elders are handicapped.

MEDICARE

Medicare was established about 25 years ago and has become one of the most popular and expensive federal programs for the aged. In 1986 it cost over $64 billion (U.S. Special Senate Committee on Aging, 1988). Part A is compulsory hospital insurance financed through Social Security taxes and Part B is a voluntary supplementary medical insurance program financed through monthly premiums and general revenues.

Unfortunately, Medicare is available only to persons over 65 and to the disabled. Thus it is a good example of positive ageism that is highly beneficial to most elders. The ageism in the program could be eliminated if the insurance were extended to all ages.

Medicaid, in contrast to Medicare, is not an ageist program because it is available to "medically indigent" persons of all ages.

The ill-fated Medicare Catastrophic Coverage Act is an example of the troubles an age-based program can run into. It was passed in November, 1988, with great fanfare. It provided medical insurance coverage against "catastrophic" (expensive) illnesses for all elders. But when elders realized that it would be financed entirely by a surtax on elders alone (and mostly on affluent elders), so many affluent elders protested that it was repealed one year later, in November, 1989.

HANDICAPPED

Most rehabilitation programs for the handicapped tend to discriminate against elders. The problem is that rehabilitation services such as physical therapy tend to be tied to employment prospects, and most disabled elders are assumed to be retired and therefore ineligible for such services (Atchley, 1988). Physicians, social workers, and others serving the handicapped do not usually refer handicapped elders for rehabilitation and occupational training programs. Because of such ageism, handicapped elders have even less access to American society than do younger handicapped people.

LONG-TERM CARE

There are two main types of long-term care for elders: nursing homes and home health care. In 1985, about 1.4 million older Americans were living in nursing homes and about 5.2 million were living in the community and needing some form of long-term care (U.S. Senate Special Committee on Aging, 1985).

Ageism is involved in long-term care in several ways. Some older people are put into nursing homes or other institutions primarily because there is no one in the community who will care for them at home. It has been estimated that up to one-third of the residents of institutions could be cared for at home as well as, or better than, they are in institutions if there were someone willing to do so and if there were proper community support services available (Estes, 1983; Markson, Levitz, & Gognalons-Caillard, 1973).

Much of this aversion to caregiving for impaired elders is due to ageism (Levin & Levin, 1980). Many assume that caring for elderly patients is difficult, disagreeable, and depressing.

Furthermore, the social organization of nursing homes (with patients at the bottom of the hierarchy) tends to promote neglect and abuse of elderly patients:

1. Patients are relatively powerless, low-status individuals whose prognosis is regarded as poor, and whose credibility is low.
2. Turnover, absenteeism, and poor role performance are common among employees who occupy marginal positions in the labor market, and such workers staff many positions in nursing homes.
3. Treatment is seen as custodial rather than as therapeutic. (Stannard, 1973, p. 329)

Just as "architecture for the elderly" is a misnomer, "homes for elders" or "retirement homes" are misnomers. These homes really are homes for the handicapped or disabled who need some personal care or congregate facilities. Here again we have the equating of "aged" with "disabled," which reinforces the negative stereotypes of old age.

AGEISM AMONG HEALTH PROFESSIONALS

All studies of health professionals' attitudes toward elders agree that they tend to have the same ageist attitudes that the rest of our society shares (Quinn, 1987a). Despite the availability of dozens of geriatric fellowships, applicants are few and several medical schools have not been able to fill some of their vacancies. Apparently extensive professional training does not correct the misconceptions and stereotypes that are so common in our culture.

There are several reasons for this. Health professionals have had little education about normal aging processes. They may know more about pathology and disease among the aged, but not about normal physical, psychological, and social aging (Palmore, 1988).

Second, they tend to share a strong fear of death, which they associate with elders (May, 1982; Vickio & Cavanaugh, 1985). Third, they have a biased experience with elders because they tend to see and treat only the most frail, sick, and senile aged. After a few years of such negative experiences, they forget that they rarely see normal healthy elders, and they begin to assume that most elders are like their sick patients.

Fourth, professionals' feelings about their own parents or older relatives can conflict with their dealings with an elderly patient (Schonfield, 1982).

As a result, physicians tend to label elders as resistant to treatment, rigid in outlook, demanding, and uninteresting. They tend to assess elderly narrowly and to prescribe medical solutions for their problems, when some of these problems might be better resolved through nonmedical means (such as a homemaker or social worker). Physicians also tend to overlook psychological disorders in elders or misdiagnose them as physical ailments (Waxman & Carner, 1984).

Nurses also have negative stereotypes about geriatric patients: their recovery is slow, they suffer from general deterioration, they are uninteresting, and they require extra nursing time for regular tasks (Carr, 1982; Olsen, 1982).

These negative attitudes can interfere with the healing process. Patients may reflect the negative expectations, believe that improvement is impossible, and so lack the motivation necessary for recovery (Olsen, 1982).

Another result of these negative attitudes is that most health professionals would rather not work with older patients. Few specialize in geriatrics and nursing home care, which results in a shortage of qualified professionals to care for elders.

Elias Cohen has recently (1988) concluded that the autonomy of elderly people with disabilities is constrained by ageism in the form of low goal formulation and underestimated potentials for self-realization and full participation in society. He states:

> American ageism is focused upon the elderly with disabilities, as opposed to the well elderly, and further, that the elderly themselves have concluded that when disability arrives, hope about continued growth, self-realization, and full participation in family and society must be abandoned so that all energy can be directed to avoiding the ultimate defeat, which is not death, but institutionalization, which is regarded as living death. (p. 25)

SETTING LIMITS ON HEALTH CARE

Recently there have been proposals to "ration" health care to elders. These proposals are based on the following considerations: federal expenditures for health care have risen rapidly from 1 percent of total federal expenditures in 1962 to 10 percent of expenditures in 1980 (Laurie, 1987). Projections indicate that this rapid increase will continue unless something is done.

Much of this expenditure is on terminally ill elders. It has been estimated that health care costs of elders who are not terminally ill are not much greater than those of middle-aged persons and that terminally ill elders consume nine times as much health care as the non-terminally ill. (Maddox, Abolafia, & Glass, 1985). Many terminal patients who are in great pain and/or do not want to prolong the dying process are being kept alive at extraordinary expense. Therefore, a reduction of medical care for these elders would substantially reduce overall medical costs.

One proposal would limit the amount of health care paid for by the government when the patient is very old, is in a terminal condition, and/or has a poor "quality of life" remaining (Callahan, 1987). Callahan argues that "medical need" no longer works as an allocation principle, because modern technology has made it too elastic a concept. There is an almost limitless amount of medical care that many people of all ages could absorb and perhaps benefit from.

He argues that age is a legitimate basis for rationing medical care because it is a meaningful, objective, precise, and universal category that does not discriminate between various social groups. This is the part of the proposal that is ageist. While using age as a basis for rationing medical care may not discriminate against other social groups, it is by definition discrimination against age groups.

The rest of Callahan's proposals are not necessarily ageist. For example, one might establish a policy of setting limits on medical care for terminal patients *regardless of age* and this would not be ageism.

Recent court cases have raised the question of whether the decision to continue life-prolonging medical treatment should be made by the patient, the family, the physicians, or the courts; as well as the question of what criteria should influence this decision (Kart, Metress, & Metress, 1988). This is especially problematic for demented or otherwise mentally incompetent patients. However, ageism is involved only if the person's age is used as a relevant factor in the decision.

HOSPICE

Hospice care is often recommended for patients irretrievably in the dying process when (1) no treatment will significantly alter the patient's disease, (2) the disease is progressive, (3) time until death is expected to be short, and (4) the intention is not to prolong dying (U.S. Department of Health, Education, and Welfare, 1983). Hospice care is directed toward simply making the patient comfortable and avoids expensive or painful treatments. Such care may be given in the home or in hospice units outside the home. It may now be paid for by Medicare and Medicaid.

One of the motivations for hospice services is to reduce the costs of terminal care. However, the cost effectiveness of such care is unclear and, depending on the services offered, may be no cheaper than traditional care (Haber, 1987). On the other hand, there is general agreement that the quality of life remaining to patients in hospice care is superior to that which patients in traditional care experience.

Hospice care would involve ageism only if age rather than prognosis is used as a criteria for recommending it. This becomes a complex issue because age may influence the prognosis given.

SUMMARY

Age-segregated housing may be preferred by some elders because of lower crime rates and easy access to services and facilities. However, the cost to elders of age-segregated housing may include feelings of isolation and neglect; and the costs to younger persons may include deprivation from normal interaction and affection from elders, loss of knowledge about aging, and loss of services from elders. In general, age-segregation tends to reinforce ageism.

Subsidized housing for elders is an example of positive ageism, because younger people are not eligible for it. It is questionable whether government funds should be used for such a program that discriminates against younger people.

"Architecture for the elderly" and "homes for elders" are really euphemisms for special housing for handicapped aged. This equating of old age with handicaps tends to reinforce ageism.

Next to Social Security retirement benefits, Medicare is the biggest and most expensive example of positive ageism. This ageism could be eliminated by extending it to cover all ages, just as Medicaid does.

Rehabilitation programs, on the other hand, tend to discriminate against elders, because elders are usually thought of as being retired and therefore not eligible.

Ageism may be involved when elders are put in institutions primarily because they are old and frail and no one will care for them in the community. Also the social organization of nursing homes tends to promote neglect and abuse of elderly patients.

Health professionals tend to share the same negative stereotypes about elders that nonprofessionals do. In addition, they tend to think that older patients are resistant to treatment, rigid, uninteresting, and demanding. As a result, most would rather not work with older patients, which causes a shortage of qualified professionals in geriatric care.

Recent proposals to limit health care are ageist insofar as these proposals are restricted to elders. Ageism may also be involved in decisions to withdraw life-prolonging medical treatment from comatose or mentally incompetent patients merely because of their advanced age.

Part IV
Reducing Ageism

12

Changing the Person

Old age is the consummation of life, just as of a play.

Cicero

It's no sin to be seventy.

Golda Meir

VARIABLES TO CONSIDER

We have reviewed the concepts and meanings of ageism, its causes and consequences, and its institutional patterns. Now we will discuss various methods of reducing ageism. In order to decide which methods are best in which situations, we need to consider (1) the goals we wish to achieve, (2) the persons to be affected, and (3) the situations to which the strategy is to be applied.

We will assume that the general goal is to reduce prejudice and discrimination toward elders. We recognize that there are competing assumptions and values in American culture which would support various kinds of ageism, especially positive ageism. But for the purposes of these chapters we assume agreement with the goal of reducing all forms of ageism.

Within this general goal we need to decide if we wish to focus on reducing ageism in individuals or in the structure of society. If we focus on reducing prejudice in individuals, then methods such as education, propaganda, personal contact, and therapy are most appropriate. These methods will be the subject of the present chapter. They may be used to reduce negative and/or positive prejudice, but we will deal mainly with negative prejudice since that seems to be the more harmful type.

If, however, we focus on reducing discrimination in the social structure, then methods such as boycotts, petitions, demonstrations, political action, legislation, and legal actions are more appropriate. These methods will be the subject of the next two chapters.

However, prejudice and discrimination are usually connected, so that reducing individual prejudice is one important way of reducing discrimination (but see next section for exceptions). It is ironic that most of the *positive* discrimination (such as Medicare) is produced by *negative* prejudice (such as the stereotypes that most aged are sick and poor).

Other variables should also be considered in devising strategy. What has been the history of this form of ageism? Is it a recent development or is it well entrenched with a long tradition behind it? Is it clearly in violation of democratic principles or is it a debatable practice with reasonable arguments in favor of it? Does the legal pattern support or allow it, or is it in violation of the law? Who benefits from it and who loses? Each of these factors may affect which strategy would be most effective.

TYPES OF PERSONS

Two generations ago Robert Merton (1949) devised a useful classification of persons in relation to racism. A different strategy is appropriate for the four different types. The following is a revised version as it applies to ageism. Table 12.1 presents a simplified diagram of these four types.

1. *The Unprejudiced Nondiscriminators.* These are the "all-weather" liberals who thoroughly accept the American creed in both belief and action. Such people should be the leaders of effective campaigns to reduce ageism.

However, their force may be reduced by the "fallacy of unanimity." This is the illusion of consensus in the community produced by the tendency of liberals to talk only to each other. When they assume unanimity on these issues, they tend to become complacent and inactive. This tendency may be overcome by de-

Table 12.1 Types of Ageists

	No discrimination	Discrimination
No prejudice	1. Unprejudiced nondiscriminator	2. Unprejudiced discriminator
Prejudice	3. Prejudiced nondiscriminator	4. Prejudiced discriminator

liberately joining groups that have prejudiced people in them and by deliberately discussing the issue with nonliberals.

2. *The Unprejudiced Discriminators.* These are the "fair-weather liberals" who despite their own lack of prejudice, support discrimination against or for elders if it is easier or profitable. These people may go along with a policy of discrimination against elders in employment so as to avoid stirring up trouble, or to secure their own promotion or other personal advantage. These people may suffer from some degree of guilt and are therefore strategic persons for the all-weather liberal to work on.

3. *The Prejudiced Nondiscriminators.* These are the "fair-weather ageists" who reluctantly conform to laws or other pressures against age discrimination. These people can be kept from discrimination, not by appeal to their democratic values, but by making discrimination costly or unpleasant. Or they may be persuaded by education and propaganda to reduce their prejudice against elders and thus move toward Type 1, the all-weather liberal.

4. *The Prejudiced Discriminators.* These are the "all-weather ageists" who are consistent in belief and practice. Strategy in dealing with these people depends on the issue and the situation. If their discrimination can be made costly through legislation or boycotts, they may move into Type 3. If they can be educated or persuaded to give up their prejudices they may be moved into Type 2 or even Type 1.

TESTING AGEISM

In order to determine which type of person one is dealing with there needs to be some kind of test or set of criteria. Quick assessment of the basic misconceptions underlying prejudice toward elders has been fairly well standardized by extensive use of the Facts on Aging Quizzes (See Appendix A and Palmore, 1988). In addition to assessing misconceptions, these quizzes can be used to indirectly measure attitudes or bias. However, other methods, such as the semantic differential method (Rosencranz & McNevin, 1969), are more accurate and more direct measures of attitudes.

Furthermore, some assessment of actual discrimination would be useful. This might be done through interviews dealing with the extent to which the subject seeks or avoids interaction with elders; discriminates for or against elders when they are at their job, when they are voting, when they are in their clubs, churches, or synagogues, and so on.

EDUCATION, PROPAGANDA, AND EXHORTATION

These methods may be used to reduce prejudice and/or discrimination. Simpson and Yinger (1985) have made useful distinctions between these methods.

Education is the transmission of noncontroversial information, or the handling of controversial topics by recognizing them as controversial, using an objective approach, and bringing all relevant facts to bear.

Propaganda, in contrast, is the manipulation of symbols on a controversial topic when the controversial element is disguised, emotional appeals are used, some or all of the relevant facts are left out or distorted, and the motives of the propagandist and/or the source of propaganda are hidden. Much of advertising uses propaganda techniques.

Exhortation is midway between education and propaganda. It often minimizes the controversial nature of the topic and uses emotional appeals; but it frequently marshals a great many facts and makes no effort to disguise its motives or its sources.

General education does appear to be effective in reducing misconceptions and ignorance about elders. In the many surveys of knowledge about aging using the Facts on Aging Quiz, the one consistent variable associated with greater knowledge has been years of education (Palmore, 1988). Also, several before-and-after tests of this knowledge have found that classes and workshops on gerontology do tend to reduce misconceptions and ignorance in this area. Thus, even short term education in gerontology reduces prejudice against elders.

Exhortation has been widely used in attempts to reduce racism (Simpson & Yinger, 1985). Typically appeals are based on religious or philosophical ideals of brotherhood, democracy, and equal opportunity. Such appeals are often modernized versions of old-fashioned sermons. Studies of the effect of such methods on racism are ambiguous (Crawford, 1974).

However, exhortation may have some impact in reducing personal ageism. It may help to reduce prejudice against elders, particularly by increasing the enthusiasm of those who are already convinced that such prejudice is wrong. It may also inhibit discrimination against elders of many fair-weather ageists (Type 3) who do not want to openly violate community norms against discrimination.

Propaganda has also been widely used to combat racism. Attempts to measure the effectiveness of such propaganda have concluded:

> Propaganda is most effective when dealing with a poorly informed audience, when it has a monopoly in the field of communication, and when it either is working in an area in which the values and needs of the public are diffuse and poorly structured or ties its appeals closely to well-structured needs and values. (Simpson & Yinger, 1985, p. 388)

Applying these criteria to ageism, it would appear that propaganda should be fairly effective (although one might choose to avoid propaganda because of the distortion and hidden motivation involved). Certainly most people are poorly informed about aging. Propaganda against ageism would not have a monopoly in communication, but organized counterpropaganda appears unlikely or relatively weak. The values and needs of the public in this area appear to be diffuse and poorly structured.

The best way to find out how effective such propaganda would be is to develop several large scale experiments to test it out. I know of no such experiments as yet.

SLOGANS

Slogans may be used in exhortation or propaganda. They have often been an important part of many movements or campaigns. In the War of Independence it was "No taxation without representation." In the Spanish-American War it was "Remember the Maine." In World War II it was "Remember Pearl Harbor." In the civil rights movement there was "Black is beautiful," "Black power," and "We shall overcome." In the feminist movement, there is "A man of quality is not threatened by a woman of equality" and "A woman's place is in the House, and the Senate."

Some pro-aged slogans have begun to appear on bumper stickers, buttons, birthday napkins, T-shirts, caps, and elsewhere. Some examples:

Age is a matter of the mind. If you don't mind, it don't matter.
Aged for smoothness and taste.
Aged to perfection.
Aging is living.
The best wines come in old bottles.
Better over the hill than under it.
Better sixty than pregnant.
Elders have done it longer.
Fifty is nifty.
Gray power.
Grow old with me, the best is yet to be.
I'm not a dirty old man. I'm a sexy senior citizen.
I'm not over the hill. I'm on a roll.
It's not how old you are, but how you are old.
Old age is better than its alternative.
Old age is not for sissies.
Old wines and violins are the best.
Older is bolder.
Over the hill and loving it.
Over the hill and off the pill.
Retired: no boss, no worries, no work, no pay.
Retired: rejuvenated, retreaded, relaxed, remodeled.
Senior power.
The first forty years are just a rehearsal.
The older the violin, the sweeter the music.
There may be snow on the roof, but there's fire in the hearth.
Things of quality have no fear of time.
When you're over the hill, you pick up speed.
Youth is a gift of nature. Age is a work of art.

To the extent that such slogans could be popularized, they could play a role in creating more positive images of aging.

ADVANTAGES OF OLD AGE

There are numerous advantages of being old that most people do not think about. Most people are more aware of the disadvantages of old age. If the advantages of old age were emphasized through education, exhortation, and propaganda, it would tend to counteract the negative stereotypes of ageing.

There are two types of advantages: those that primarily benefit society and those that primarily benefit the older person (Palmore, 1979). There are five characteristics of elders that benefit society.

1. *More law-abiding*. It is clear that older persons are more law-abiding, regardless of how it is measured (Chapter 9).

2. *More political participation*. Elders are better citizens also in that they vote more frequently, are more interested and informed about public issues, contact public officials more often, and more often serve in public office. When sex and socioeconomic status are controlled, persons over 65 have the highest voting rate of any age group (Atchley, 1987b).

3. *More voluntary activities*. Most aged also serve society through maintaining or increasing their participation in voluntary organizations and churches. Several studies have shown that when socioeconomic differences and health are controlled, elders continue or increase voluntary activities (Cutler, 1987).

4. *Better workers*. Despite widespread beliefs to the contrary, most studies of older workers agree that in most jobs older workers perform as well or better than younger workers on most measures (Chapter 2).

5. *Greater wisdom*. There is no scientific evidence that elders as a group are wiser than younger people. This is because no one has yet developed an objective, valid, and reliable measure of wisdom. However, insofar as wisdom is dependent on years of experience and the maturity that comes from experience, it seems probable that elders tend to be wiser than younger people.

There are at least a dozen advantages that primarily benefit the older person. Some of these advantages result from positive ageism, but are advantages in our society nevertheless.

1. *Less criminal victimization*. In addition to being more law-abiding, elders are less often victims of crime. Contrary to popular opinion, persons over 65 have substantially lower victimization rates in nearly all categories of crime (Chapter 9).

2. *Fewer accidents.* The aged also suffer less accidents than any other age group. Their accident rate is less than two-thirds that of all persons (National Center for Health Statistics, 1977). Their accident rate is also lower in each category: motor vehicle, work, home, and other accidents. Similarly, older drivers have safer driving records than those under age 65 (National Safety Council, 1981).

3. *Social Security and other pensions.* This is the most important economic advantage of elders. The pensions make it possible for most elders to retire with almost as much (if not more) disposable income as they had before retirement (Palmore et al., 1985). A special advantage of Social Security and other government pensions is that they are now inflation-proof; their benefits automatically increase with the cost-of-living index.

4. *Supplemental Security Income.* In 1974 the SSI program established what is essentially a guaranteed minimum income for all persons over age 65 (as well as the blind and disabled). In 1987 persons over 65 could receive monthly payments of up to $340 for an individual and $510 for a couple.

5. *Lower taxes.* There are numerous tax benefits that only elders can enjoy, such as extra personal exemptions for those using standard deductions, exemptions of Social Security income from taxation, reduced property taxes, and exemption of capital gains from sale of personal residence.

6. *Medicare.* Elders are the only age group who have national health insurance. They received about $63 billion in health benefits from Medicare in 1985 (Hudson, 1987).

7. *Free services and reduced rates.* The various free or reduced rate programs and services provided specially for older people by the federal and state governments or by private agencies are too numerous to list here, but they include the following major ones: housing, meals, drug discounts, transportation, entertainment, education, information, referral, planning, coordination, employment counseling, and day care.

8. *Freedom from child rearing.* Most elders no longer have any child rearing responsibilities. This frees them from both the financial drain of supporting children and the physical and psychological strain of caring for children. This freedom releases time, money, and energy for whatever the elder wants to do.

9. *Freedom from pregnancy.* Similarly, elders do not need to fear unwanted pregnancies and all the difficult decisions about abortion, adoption, or keeping an unwanted child that such preg-

nancies entail. Many elders report enhanced sexual enjoyment because of the release from this fear. This advantage is reflected in the slogans "Over the hill and off the pill" and "Better over the hill than pregnant."

10. *Freedom from work.* Most elders are retired and those few who continue to be employed (about 12%) tend to work at part-time or temporary jobs. This too releases large amounts of time and energy for whatever the elder wants to do. Furthermore, legislation now prohibits age discrimination in employment, so that elders now have more freedom to work if they wish to.

11. *Less mental illness.* Contrary to popular opinion, elders have lower rates of mental illness when all the major illnesses are added together (Myers et al., 1984).

12. *Less alcoholism and drug abuse.* Fewer elders suffer from these addictions than any other adult age group (Kastenbaum, 1987; Whittington, 1987). This is an advantage both to the elders themselves and to the society because of the great personal and social costs of these addictions.

It should be understood that we are not arguing that these advantages necessarily outweigh the obvious disadvantages of aging in our society. That is a complex value judgment that each individual must make—and the decision will, of course, depend heavily on one's own experience with aging. We are suggesting that more emphasis on these advantages through education, exhortation, and propaganda can help to reduce unwarranted fears of aging and negative images of elders.

CHURCHES AND SYNAGOGUES

Religious organizations are uniquely able to use exhortation to reduce ageism. First, they can influence more people than any other type of institution.

Second, they can call on the authority of the Bible and other teachings of their religion to oppose ageism. Since the mid-1970s the major denominations' statements on aging contain affirmations of the value and dignity of every person regardless of age, and the commandment to honor and respect the elderly (Payne, 1984). These statements affirm aging as a part of God's created order; confirm the Biblical perspective of old age as life transformed, renewed, and filled with blessings and opportunities; and affirm that older people are to be respected, honored, and regarded as skilled resources for church lay ministry.

The Jewish tradition reveres elders because they represent life's fulfillment and the wisdom of experience. Disrespect for elders is said to be indicative of a corrupt generation. Respect for age was expressed in the directive "Thou shalt rise before the hoary head and honor the face of the old man." Accordingly, one should not sit in the seat of an old person, speak before he has spoken, or contradict him (Kahana & Kahana, 1985).

The danger of such teachings is that they may go too far and encourage positive ageism. But this is a danger in all attempts to overcome prejudice against elders.

THE MEDIA

Television, newspapers, magazines, comic books, and other mass media could be powerful agents to combat negative stereotypes about elders. They could intentionally show older people with normal or positive attributes. Instead of stories on poor elderly in miserable nursing homes, there could be stories about affluent elders in the community active in community affairs. Instead of stories about elderly victims of crime, there could be stories about elders who mount a community crime watch to deter criminal activity.

Instead of articles on health problems of elderly, there could be articles on how to maintain health and fitness throughout life. Instead of alarming statistics on how much poverty there is among elders, there could be more realistic statistics on how affluent the majority are and what a potential market they are for various products and services.

There are now many 16 mm films, videocassettes, and audiocassettes about aging and the aged that were designed to decrease ageism and increase accurate knowledge about elders. *The Gerontologist* reviews several of these in each issue. These could be more widely used by educational and religious institutions, civic groups, libraries, television, and radio stations to reduce ageism.

The danger of such approaches is that they may produce opposite and positive stereotypes, which are just as unrealistic and rigid. A realistic balance between positive and negative images is necessary to prevent this.

If we review the classic characteristics of stereotypes (Simpson & Yinger, 1985), we can see how the media could combat them:

1. *The stereotype gives a highly exaggerated picture of the importance of a few characteristics.* The media could present less exaggerated images and deemphasize the importance of these characteristics. For example, a common stereotype is that most elders have major problems with "aging skin" (wrinkles, sagging, blemishes, liver spots, moles, cancers, etc.). In fact, only a few elders have major dermatological problems and these rarely interfere with functioning.

2. *Some stereotypes are invented with no basis in fact, and are made to seem reasonable by association with other tendencies that have a kernel of truth.* For example, the widespread stereotype that most elders are senile is made to seem reasonable by the association of senility with Alzheimer's disease, which does increase in old age. The media could point out that Alzheimer's disease is actually uncommon among elders (only about 2% to 6%: Cohen, 1987) and that elders actually have less mental illness when all types are considered.

3. *In a negative stereotype, favorable characteristics are either omitted entirely or insufficiently stressed.* The media could balance negative characteristics of elders with some positive ones, such as the advantages of aging discussed above.

4. *The stereotype fails to show how the majority share the same tendencies or have other undesirable characteristics.* For example, the stereotypes that elders have impairments of memory, mobility, hearing, vision, and so on, fail to show that many younger people also have these impairments. Similarly, they do not recognize that younger people have *more* impairments due to mental illness, drug addiction, alcoholism, and so on. The media could balance its negative images of aging with more negative images of younger people.

5. *Stereotypes fail to give any attention to the cause of the tendencies of the minority group—particularly to the role of the majority itself and its stereotypes in creating the very characteristics being condemned.* For example, the inactivity of many elders is partly produced by forced retirement and other discrimination against elders, which are based on the stereotypes that most elders are useless or lazy. The media could point out how discrimination against elders encourages inactivity.

6. *Stereotypes leave little room for change; there is a lag in keeping up with the tendencies that actually typify many members of a group.* For example, the stereotypes that most elders are poor, sick, or senile, do not recognize that there have been substantial improvements in these areas during the past generation. The media

could bring people up-to-date with information about these recent improvements.

7. *Stereotypes leave little room for individual variation, which is particularly wide among elders.* The media could point out that elders are as varied as younger persons, if not more so. It could show that elders are some of the richest *and* poorest, some of the most athletic *and* most incapacitated, some of the most brilliant *and* most disoriented, and so on, people in society.

PERSONAL CONTACT

Simpson & Yinger (1985) assert,

> No factor has received more attention among strategies for reducing prejudice and discrimination than the effects of contact between the members of different groups. It is often said, "If there were only more contact, if people only knew each other better, there would be less prejudice." Yet it is also known that prejudice often seems most intense in areas where there is most contact. (p. 390)

For example, it is well known in the area of race relations that unequal-status contact, in which the dominant group member has superior status to the minority group member (as in a master-slave relationship), tends to reinforce prejudice rather than reduce it. It is only equal-status contacts, or ones that disconfirm stereotypes, that tend to reduce prejudice.

Therefore, unequal-status contact with elders that reinforces stereotypes may actually increase ageism rather than reduce it. For example, visits to nursing homes usually reinforce the stereotype that most elders are sick or senile.

On the other hand, visits to an exercise class or health spa for elders would tend to undermine the stereotype that most elders are sick. Similarly, visits to a continuing education class for elders would undermine the stereotype that most elders are senile.

Another problem with personal contacts, even if they are between people with equal statuses, is that they may involve competition or conflict. When the contact is competitive or antagonistic, it tends to reinforce prejudice (Simpson & Yinger, 1985). For example, competition between older and younger workers for scarce jobs during high unemployment could increase prejudice and hostility against elders.

In contrast, when the contact involves working together for a common goal (on an equal-status basis), contact tends to reduce prejudice. Thus, intergenerational projects or committees, in which older and younger persons need to cooperate in order to achieve their goals, should be an effective way to reduce prejudice between the generations.

EXAMPLES THAT BREAK STEREOTYPES

There are many elders who break stereotypes through their personal example. Millions of healthy, strong, and athletic elders break the stereotype of illness and disability. The Senior Olympic Games involve thousands of athletes who often perform better than most younger people. There were even three men over the age of 90 who ran the New York City Marathon in 1989, and more than 400 runners were over age 60 (*New York Times*, 1989)!

Some elders break the stereotype of physical decline by birthday feats that show their *increasing* physical ability. "Hardrock Simpson" of Burlington, North Carolina, was a mail carrier who ran his age in miles each year on his birthday until he was over 90. Waldo Henninger of Sun City, Arizona, swam his age in laps in the Sun City pool (nonstop) until he was over 90.

I have been inspired by these men to ride my age in miles on my bicycle, and do my age in knee-bends, push-ups, sit-ups, and toe-touches on my birthday. I have been doing this for about 20 years. It was not too difficult to do 60 miles, knee-bends, push-ups, sit-ups, and toe-touches on my sixtieth birthday, but I expect it will become difficult to do 90 of these when I am 90! There are many other examples of elders who break stereotypes. The millions of older couples who continue to enjoy their sexual activity break the stereotype of impotency.

The thousands of scientists, authors, musicians, artists, professors, business executives, and other distinguished elders who continue to be creative late in life break the stereotype of mental decline and senility.

The millions of older workers who continue to be productive and efficient either through paid employment or volunteer work break the stereotype of uselessness.

The stereotype of isolation is broken by the vast majority of elders who maintain their social networks or even increase their social activities because of their greater leisure time.

The thousands of older millionaires and the millions of elders who are more affluent than they ever were in younger life break the stereotype of poverty.

The millions of happy elders who say "These are the best years of my life" break the stereotype of depression and misery.

Many elders intentionally behave in ways that contradict ageist stereotypes, partly because they want to challenge these stereotypes. They engage in athletics, dancing, productivity, creativity, and leadership partly to show that these things can be done in old age.

THERAPY

Insofar as ageism is a manifestation of personal insecurities or personality instability (see Chapter 4), a reduction of these disturbances would tend to reduce ageism. Furthermore, prevention of such disturbances through conditions that encourage mental health in general is more effective than attempts to cure mental illness after it has occurred.

Personal therapy can range from friendly counseling to intensive psychoanalysis, but is most effective in reducing prejudice when individuals are helped to face the causes of their prejudices.

However, the best individual therapy suffers from two disadvantages: it is costly in time and energy, and it fails to reduce group support for prejudice. Group therapy attempts to overcome these disadvantages. It is less costly in terms of professional time because one therapist can treat several people in a group simultaneously. Secondly, it uses the effects of group dynamics to change personalities and reduce prejudices.

Some successful experiments have been done with group therapy to reduce race and ethnic prejudices (Simpson & Yinger, 1985), and such techniques might be used to reduce ageism also.

SUMMARY

In considering various strategies to reduce ageism, we need to consider the types of goals, persons, and situations involved. This chapter focuses on methods for reducing prejudice in individuals.

There are four types of persons: the unprejudiced nondiscriminators, the unprejudiced discriminators, the prejudiced nondiscriminators, and the prejudiced discriminators. The first type is subject to the fallacy of unanimity, which tends to produce complacency and inaction. Unprejudiced discriminators are a strategic type to work on, because they may suffer from guilt about the discrepancy between their beliefs and actions. The prejudiced non-discriminators may also feel strain because of the discrepancy between their prejudiced beliefs and their lack of discrimination. The prejudiced discriminators are the most difficult to deal with because they need reductions in both prejudice and discrimination.

In order to determine which type of person one is dealing with, tests or other indicators of ignorance, prejudice, and discrimination are required. Then one may use education, propaganda, or exhortation depending on the needs, resources, and situation. There have been experiments showing that education can be effective in reducing misconceptions about aging, but there has been little research on the effectiveness of exhortation and propaganda against ageism. One popular form of pro-aged propaganda are the slogans printed on T-shirts, bumper stickers, and buttons.

There are five advantages of old age that benefit society: elders are more law-abiding; more politically active; more active in voluntary activities; are better workers; and may have more wisdom. There are advantages that primarily benefit the older person: elders have less criminal victimization and less accidents; have Social Security and other pensions; have a guaranteed minimum income and lower taxes; have Medicare and other free services; have freedom from child rearing, from pregnancy, and from work; have less mental illness, and less alcoholism and drug abuse. More emphasis on these advantages could help reduce prejudice against elders.

Religious organizations are uniquely able to use exhortation to reduce ageism, because most people belong to one and because they can call on the authority of the Bible and other teachings of their religion.

The media could also be powerful agents to combat prejudice against elders. It could reduce negative stereotypes by deemphasizing exaggerated problems, presenting facts about misconceptions, emphasizing positive characteristics and advantages of aging, pointing out that many younger persons have the same problems, showing how discrimination can produce negative characteristics in elders, showing how the characteristics of elders have improved in recent years, and pointing out the wide individual variation among elders.

Personal contact is most effective in reducing prejudice when it is between equal status persons in a cooperative relationship. Personal therapy may be effective in reducing ageism insofar as it is caused by mental disturbances. Group therapy is less costly and can utilize group dynamics to reduce prejudice.

The next chapter will discuss how ageism could be reduced in various institutions.

13

Changing the Structure

It is my thesis that in many technologically, medically, and socially advanced societies, trends of a new valorization of older people have set in.

Rosenmayr, 1987

By and large, other countries have favored the creation of public universal systems of service provision rather than ones focused categorically on specific age groups, such as the elderly.

Nusberg, 1984

THE ECONOMY

Negative Discrimination in Employment

Legislation has gone almost as far as it can go toward eliminating discrimination against elders in employment. The Age Discrimination in Employment Acts now prohibit such discrimination in most federal, state, and private jobs. The act does exempt college faculty, firefighters, and police, but these exemptions are due to expire in 1993.

However, even after 1993 it will still allow mandatory retirement based on age for elected public officials, their staff and advisors not covered by civil service, as well as for executives with pension benefits of over $44,000. Furthermore, employers are permitted to discriminate against elders if they can show that age is a bona fide requirement for employment. The Federal Aviation Administration currently requires retirement of commercial airline pilots at age 60.

The rationale for allowing mandatory retirement in these occupations appears to be that it is difficult, if not impossible, to fairly evaluate continuing competence in such high level positions, and that therefore age may be used as a "proxy indicator" of declining competence.

I would argue that the difficulties of fairly evaluating competence in such occupations are far outweighed by the dangers of forcing competent and creative people to retire from these occupations just because of their age. The only thing that can be said in favor of age as an indicator of competence is that it is objective. Experts agree that in every other respect it is a poor indicator of any kind of competence in any occupation. Therefore, legislation could be passed to close these remaining loopholes for ageism in the Age Discrimination in Employment Acts.

However, because many more elders would be affected, it is more important to vigorously enforce the legislation now on the books, to mount campaigns designed to reduce employers' prejudices against older workers, and to impress employers with the penalties they face for illegal employment discrimination.

The Commonwealth Fund has recently embarked on an Older Americans at Work Program designed to work with business to improve employment opportunities for older Americans. This is an example of how private foundations and other organizations can reduce the ageism against older workers and increase their employment opportunities.

Positive Discrimination in Employment. As pointed out in Chapter 8, older age appears to be an advantage in a few high level occupations such as judges, senators, and presidents of organizations. But we concluded that this is probably caused less by prejudice in favor of old age than by the assumption that more experience tends to bring more wisdom and other skills relevant to the occupations. In either case, it appears impractical and/or undesirable to do much about this advantage.

More serious in their impact on younger people are the federal employment programs for low income elders. Workers of all ages must pay for these programs, but younger people are barred from participating in them. A simple way to eliminate such ageism would be to open these programs to workers of all ages.

Social Security Retirement Benefits

This massive program is a form of positive ageism because it is available only to those over 62. One way to eliminate this ageism would be to change the eligibility criteria from years of age to years of contribution (say 40 years) to the program. Thus, those who started working earlier could retire earlier than those who started working later. This would be more equitable than the present system in which everyone has to wait until the same age before retiring, regardless of how many years they have contributed to Social Security.

In order to avoid penalizing those who have been homemakers for much of their lives, contribution credit could be given for years in which they were homemakers and not employed.

Supplemental Security Income (SSI)

This is another ageist program because it is limited to those over 65 (or disabled). This ageism could also be eliminated by changing eligibility from years of age to years of service; or SSI could be extended to all ages. If it were so extended, we would have a national guaranteed income program for all Americans.

Taxation

The tax break that excludes Social Security and Railroad Retirement benefits from the federal income tax (except for those with over $32,000 annual income, not counting Social Security) is based on the rationale that retirees have had their contribution taxed when they were employed and therefore it would amount to double taxation if the benefits from those contributions were also taxed.

The only flaw in this argument is that the *employer's* contribution was not taxed and therefore the portion of benefits derived from the employer's contribution (one-half) escapes taxation altogether. A more equitable (and less ageist) system would be to count one-half of all Social Security retirement benefits as taxable income (as is now done for those with other income that is over $32,000).

The exclusion from income tax of the capital gains on home sales (one-time only) for people 55 and over could be made nonageist by extending this exclusion to persons of all ages. This would further encourage investment in homes.

There no longer seems to be any justification for the additional exemption of $750 for an individual and $1,200 for a couple over 65 using the standard deduction. Nor is there any justification for continuing the many other income and property tax breaks given elders by state and local governments.

Not only are such tax breaks for elders ageist in nature, but they tend to favor higher income elders more than lower income elders, thus widening the gap between affluent and poor elders (Nelson, 1983). If such ageist tax breaks were eliminated we would have a more equitable taxation system.

THE GOVERNMENT

Negative Ageism in Government Programs

The ageism found by the U.S. Commission on Civil Rights (1977) in the administration of some federal programs is inconsistent with the principles of equal opportunity and fair treatment of all persons regardless of race, sex, or age. Most Americans would agree that such ageism should be eliminated.

Such ageism could be reduced by individual complaints to the administrators in charge, to state and federal representatives, and, if necessary, by legal action under the civil rights acts. When a pattern of discrimination is apparent, pressure should be brought on the offending agency to change its policies and prevent such occurrences.

Positive Ageism in Government Programs

The positive ageism shown by such programs as the Area Agencies on Aging, Public Housing, Senior Community Service Employment, Foster Grandparents, Green Thumb, Retired Seniors, and Senior Home Aides is more controversial. Indeed, they are of such benefit to elders and represent such a relatively small portion of the federal budget that there has been little criticism of them.

However, the fact that they are restricted to elders makes them ageist. This ageism could be eliminated by opening up the programs to all persons, or by creating parallel programs for younger people. The latter option would be preferred by those who argue that elders have special needs that are best served by special programs.

To some extent, this is already being done because there are special programs for children, youth, and young adults. The question remains as to whether there is equity between the generations in terms of how much money is being devoted to these programs relative to the needs of the different generations.

The arguments for and against using age as a criteria in public programs have been summarized by Neugarten (1982):

Arguments *for* using age as a criteria are:

1. Age-based federal programs have proved their effectiveness in reducing poverty among the aged and so should be used for other programs.
2. The aged are discriminated against and disadvantaged in need-based programs such as mental health services.
3. Means tests and needs tests are demeaning, difficult to administer, and costly.
4. The most appropriate time for intervention for many problems is in old age.
5. Age-categorical programs are more politically viable than need-based programs.

Arguments *against* using age as a criteria are:

1. The heterogeneity of the aged makes uniform services inappropriate and wasteful.
2. The general trend toward an age-irrelevant society makes age less relevant for services.
3. The aged have enjoyed greater reductions in poverty than other age groups and so should no longer have special income supports.
4. Emphasizing the needs and dependency of the aged as a group has a stigmatizing effect on all aged.
5. Age-based, need-irrelevant programs cause divisiveness between age categories.
6. Need-based programs have greater target efficiency.

One unavoidable problem with age-specific programs is that they are age-segregated. Age segregation, like any form of segregation, tends to produce prejudice and misunderstandings between groups. Because of this, there needs to be unusually strong reasons to justify age-specific programs instead of age-inclusive programs.

Crime

As pointed out in Chapter 9, elders generally suffer from criminal victimization less than younger people. The one exception to this generalization is in the area of fraud and medical quackery. Elders are more victimized by this type of crime because of the stereotypes of elders as gullible, ignorant, and desperate to try any possible cure of their disease. A way to reduce this kind of ageism is to educate elders about these kinds of fraud and how to protect themselves against them.

However, positive ageism on the part of some police, attorneys, juries, and judges may account for part of the very low crime rates reported for elders. There is no conclusive evidence about how widespread such discrimination is in our legal system. However, most would agree that wherever it occurs, it is a violation of the principle of equal protection by the law, and should be eliminated.

The best hope for reducing such discrimination probably lies in changing the attitudes of the key actors in the legal system so that they are less prejudiced by stereotypes that elders are kind, dependable, honest, and so on.

THE FAMILY

Marriage

The tendency of men to marry younger women is a gender-specific kind of ageism. This is a major cause of the fact that older women find it very difficult to remarry when they become divorced or widowed. This prejudice against older women could be reduced the same way other prejudices can be reduced: through education, exhortation, propaganda, the media, and equal status personal contact.

Remarriage among elders in general is discouraged by the stereotype that elders are or should be sexless. This prejudice is compounded by fears among children about loss of their inheritance if their parents remarry. Since elders tend to be sensitive to the attitudes and expectations of their children in this regard, children can play a key role in overcoming this kind of ageism by encouraging their parents to remarry.

Elder Abuse

It should be remembered that most elder abuse is not due to prejudice against elders, but to attempts at exploitation, or escape from care-giving duties, or resentment at being dependent, or revenge for being abused as a child, or to some form of mental illness (Quinn, 1987a). In order to reduce such abuse, better detection, diagnosis of the root problems, and provision of treatment and services to overcome the problems would be more effective than legislation providing stiffer penalties for abuse.

HOUSING

Residential Segregation

To the extent that age-segregated housing is due to prejudice between the generations, it can be reduced the same way other prejudice can be reduced. However, most such segregation appears to be voluntary. Therefore, the main goal in this area should be the maintenance of true freedom of choice; so that those who prefer segregated housing can have it and those who prefer integrated housing can remain in their integrated communities.

Subsidized Housing

Special housing for elders, subsidized by public funds, is by definition a kind of ageism because it discriminates against younger people. However, such housing has several laudable goals: to enable frail elderly to remain in the community and avoid unnecessary institutionalization, and to provide the special facilities and services that frail elders need.

These goals could be achieved without ageism if the special housing were open to frail persons *of all ages*. Frail younger people need special housing and services just as much as frail elders.

The provision of age-segregated housing at public expense just to provide this option for low income elders seems to be a highly controversial policy at best, and may even be contrary to federal and state regulations against discrimination and segregation.

Architecture

As pointed out in Chapter 11, architecture "for the elderly" appears to be really architecture for the handicapped. This is a kind of ageism because the equating of elderly with handicapped encourages the stereotype that most elderly are handicapped. This could be eliminated by simply changing the terminology and recognizing that such architecture is for the handicapped (or disabled, or frail, etc.).

HEALTH CARE

Medicare

This massive example of positive ageism could continue to provide its needed health care and yet eliminate its discrimination, if it were extended to all age groups. Then we would become like most other industrialized nations by having national health insurance for all ages. (South Africa is the only other industrialized nation without this.)

Handicapped

Discrimination against handicapped elders by rehabilitation programs is based on the stereotype that most elders cannot and/or do not want to be productive. Such ageism could be eliminated by giving handicapped elders equal access to rehabilitation services regardless of their age.

Long-Term Care

The ageism that forces elders into nursing homes because they are old and there is no one in the community willing to care for them, could be reduced by providing subsidies for home care and by providing adequate community services to support home care.

The ageism within nursing homes that promotes neglect and abuse of elderly patients could be reduced through education, exhortation, better supervision, better pay, and better working conditions.

Health Professionals

As pointed out in Chapter 11, the usual ageism found in most members of our society becomes compounded among health professionals with their strong fear of death, their biased experience with elders, and the difficulties of managing elderly patients within their institutions. As a result, health professionals may give poorer treatment to elderly patients. Another result is a shortage of qualified health professionals in geriatrics.

Such ageism could be reduced by better training in geriatrics and in the social and psychological facts about aging so as to counteract the negative stereotypes so common in health professionals. The U.S. Health Resources and Services Administration

(Public Health Service) is attempting to do this through its 38 Geriatric Education Centers around the nation. Special incentives to medical students and other health professionals could encourage more of them to specialize in geriatrics.

Limits on Health Care

Proposals to limit health care for terminal or frail elders, but not for similar younger people, are clearly ageist. Considering the vast amounts of money, equipment, and personnel that are spent on prolonging the life of terminally ill patients, policies limiting health care for all terminally ill patients *regardless of age* would save great amounts of resources and yet would not be ageist.

SUMMARY

Additional legislation could close the two remaining loopholes in the Age Discrimination in Employment Act, but far more important in terms of number of elders affected would be the vigorous enforcement of the act and campaigns to reduce employers' prejudices against older workers.

The ageism in federal employment programs for low income elders could be eliminated by extending the programs to cover low income workers of all ages. The ageism in Social Security Retirement Benefits could be eliminated by changing the eligibility criteria from years of age to years of contribution to the program. The ageism in the Supplemental Security Income program could be eliminated by extending it to all ages.

The exemption of Social Security benefits from taxation would be more equitable if one half of the benefits (representing the employer's contribution) were made taxable. Other tax breaks for elders could be extended to all ages or eliminated.

Discrimination against elders by government agencies could be reduced by individual complaints and legal action under the civil rights act.

The positive ageism in the many special government programs for elders could be eliminated by opening these programs to younger people. Discrimination in favor of elders in our legal system is clearly unconstitutional and should be eliminated.

Remarriage of elders in general, and especially of older women, is discouraged by various stereotypes and prejudices. Adult children can play a key role in overcoming such prejudices and encouraging remarriage.

Elder abuse can be reduced through better detection, diagnosis, and provision of treatment and services, rather than through legislation to provide stiffer penalties.

Subsidized housing for frail elders can be made nonageist by opening it up to frail persons of all ages. So called "architecture for the elderly" should be called "architecture for the handicapped," which would be more accurate and nonageist.

Medicare could be made nonageist by extending it to all ages. Discrimination against elders in rehabilitation programs should be eliminated.

Forcing elders into nursing homes because of their age and lack of caretakers in the community could be reduced by subsidies for home care and community support services. Ageism within nursing homes, which leads to neglect and abuse, is a difficult problem that requires multiple interventions.

Ageism among health professionals could be reduced by better training in geriatrics and in the social and psychological facts about aging. Limits on health care should be based on condition and cost/benefit considerations rather than on chronological age.

14

Strategies for Change

Don't agonize. Organize!

Anonymous

What can be done to reduce ageism? In general, most of the strategies that have been successful in reducing racism and sexism could be used to reduce ageism. This includes individual actions and organized actions.

INDIVIDUAL ACTIONS

The question is often raised, "What can one unimportant individual like me do to reduce such massive problems as racism, sexism, and ageism?" People who raise this question should remember that the massive deserts are made up of tiny grains of sand, each unimportant by itself.

The following is a list of individual actions derived from strategies that have been successful in reducing prejudice and discrimination of other kinds.

1. Inform yourself so you have the facts to combat the misconceptions and stereotypes.
2. Examine your own attitudes and actions and try to eliminate those that express ageism.
3. Inform your relatives, friends, and colleagues about the facts, especially when some prejudice is expressed or implied.

4. Do not tell ageist jokes and refuse to laugh when you hear one. Or change the ageist joke to one that is age-neutral by not specifying the subject's age.
5. Do not use ageist terms like "old fogy" and "old maid."
6. Do not use ageist language such as equating aging with deterioration and dying, or equating youth with health, vigor, and beauty.
7. Point out to others when they are using ageist language.
8. Refuse to go along with discrimination against adults of any age, young or old.
9. Write letters to editors of newspapers and magazines pointing out and protesting ageism in current events.
10. Write letters to local officials, state and federal representatives, and executives pointing out and protesting ageism in government. Also write letters that support legislation against ageism.
11. Boycott products of companies that use ageist advertisements or discriminate against elders in employment.
12. Join groups that oppose ageism and work with them (see next section).
13. Vote for political candidates who oppose ageism.
14. Testify before legislative committees and commissions about instances of ageism and show your support for legislation to reduce ageism.
15. Become a candidate for political office or get appointed to commissions that can reduce ageism.

ORGANIZED ACTIONS

While individual actions can make a difference, these actions become much more powerful when they are united and organized. The following are organized actions that are difficult for an individual to carry out alone, but that have been effective when carried out by an organized group.

1. Gather and disseminate information about the facts on aging in order to reduce prejudice against elders.
2. Organize public meetings with panels, lecturers, audiovisuals, and other media to inform and persuade.
3. Publish advertisements opposing ageism and supporting equal opportunity.

4. Use talk shows and other forms of mass media to educate and exhort people to oppose ageism.
5. Lobby for legislation to oppose ageism.
6. Organize a petition drive to oppose some aspect of ageism.
7. Take class action suits to court to encourage more enforcement of current laws against ageism. Help pay legal fees of individuals suing for equal opportunity.
8. Support the use of grievance procedures against the Social Security Administration, the Department of Social Services, rehabilitation agencies, and other government agencies to correct instances of ageism.
9. Organize a boycott of products from companies with ageist practices.
10. Organize a rent strike against ageist landlords.
11. Organize watchdog activities to insure that agencies do not discriminate against elders.
12. Give group support to individual activists.
13. Organize demonstrations such as marches, picketing, and public meetings.
14. Organize passive resistance and nonviolent confrontation such as mass loading of busses to show need for reduced fares, sit-ins at abandoned buildings to dramatize housing shortages, mass visits to facilities serving elders.
15. Support political campaigns for local, state, and federal officials and legislators who oppose ageism.
16. Register nursing home and retirement home residents as absentee voters.
17. Conduct voter registration drives among elders in the community.
18. Educate elders about political aspects of ageism.
19. Raise funds for campaigns against ageism.
20. Organize civil disobedience actions to protest ageism in the government or in business.
21. Enlist the cooperation of other organizations, such as churches and unions, to support campaigns against ageism.

ORGANIZATIONS OPPOSED TO AGEISM

The following is an alphabetical list of the major national organizations working to reduce negative ageism, with some comments about size and activities. Unfortunately, most of these organizations also favor special programs for elders that involve positive ageism. But as a member, one could try to eliminate their support for positive ageism.

Administration on Aging (AoA)
U.S. Department of Health and Human Services
30 Independence Ave. SW
Washington, DC 20201

The AoA aids states and communities in developing responsive systems of services for all older persons, especially those in economic need. The AoA has special interests in rural elderly, housing and environment, long-term care, health and nutrition, applied research, education and training, and the family.

American Association of Retired Persons (AARP)
1909 K Street NW
Washington, D.C. 20049

This is the nation's largest (about 30 million members) nonprofit, nonpartisan organization of Americans age 50 and older. AARP offers a wide range of membership benefits, legislative representation at the federal and state levels, and educational and community service programs which are implemented through a national network of volunteers and local chapters. Much of their legislative lobbying and educational programs are designed to reduce prejudice and discrimination against elders.

American Society on Aging (ASA)
833 Market St., Suite 516
San Francisco, CA 94103

The ASA was founded in 1954 as the Western Gerontological Society. They changed their name to the American Society on Aging in 1985. The ASA is a nonprofit professional association dedicated to enhancing the well-being of older people, disseminating information on aging, and educating and training professionals in aging.

The Association for Gerontology in Higher Education (AGHE)
600 Maryland Ave. S.W., West Wing 204
Washington, DC 20024

AGHE was established in 1974 as a membership organization of colleges and universities that provide research, education, training, and service programs in aging. It now has more than 250 member institutions. Its basic goal is to assist faculty and administrators in developing and improving the quality of gerontology programs in higher education. It combats ageism mainly through its education and advocacy programs.

Bald Headed Men of America (BHMA)
Capps Printing Company
Morehead City, NC

BHMA was established 16 years ago to combat prejudice against bald men and to prove that "bald men have more fun." They have an annual "Bald Is Beautiful" convention in Mrs. Willis' seafood restaurant in Morehead City every second weekend in September. The convention features slogans about baldness ("Save the hair—get a cigar box to keep it in!"; "Be proud of every hair you don't have"; "No drugs, no plugs, no rugs"; "Most men use their hormones to grow hair—but intelligent women know what bald men use their hormones for!"), a bald beauty contest, a bald floor show, a "Bald as a Golf Ball Tournament," and sharing of stories about "how discouraging it is to keep up the pretense that you aren't losing your hair, and how liberating it is to stop" (Crease, 1987).

Elvirita Lewis Foundation (ELF)
255 North El Cielo Rd. Shite 144
Palm Springs, CA 92262

The ELF is a nonprofit foundation and mass membership organization, which for more than a decade has promoted the philosophy of productive aging that older people are a major untapped resource in solving social problems. Thus it combats ageism through opening opportunities for employment and service by elders.

The Gerontological Society of America (GSA)
1275 K Street NW, Suite 350
Washington, DC 20005

The GSA was founded in 1945 to promote the scientific study of aging and to encourage the exchange of knowledge about aging among scientists and practitioners in the field. Today the society has over 6,000 members belonging to one of four sections: Biological Sciences; Clinical Medicine; Behavioral and Social Sciences; and Social Research, Planning, and Practice. It combats ageism mainly through research and education that challenge stereotypes about elders.

The Gray Panthers
311 South Juniper St., Suite 601
Philadelphia, PA 19107

Founded in 1970, the Gray Panthers are an intergenerational advocacy movement dedicated to promoting a positive attitude toward aging, exposing age-related inequities and injustices, influencing social policies, and organizing grassroots networks to address social issues on the community level. By 1985, more that 120 Gray Panther chapters had been established in 40 states with 8,000 local chapter members and 60,000 national members at large. They are more militant than the other organizations because they challenge stereotypes and are concerned with action for change rather than service.

National Association for Hispanic Elderly
2727 West 6th St., Suite 270
Los Angeles, CA 90057

This association is a nonprofit social service and economic development organization that places major emphasis upon research and data collection, development and management of model projects, and specialized work in media and communications dealing with Hispanic elders. Thus it opposes both ageism and ethnic discrimination.

National Caucus on Black Aged (NCBA)
1424 K St., NW, Suite 500
Washington, DC 20005

The NCBA was established in 1970 to help improve the quality and length of life for aged Blacks through political action. In 1973, federal funding enabled it to establish its National Center on Black Aged in Washington, DC. It combats both ageism and racism.

National Council of Senior Citizens (NCSC)
1511 K Street NW
Washington, DC 20005

The NCSC originated in 1961 as a pressure group to support the enactment of Medicare legislation. Its leadership has always come from labor unions, mainly the AFL-CIO and other industrial unions. It now has over 3,500,000 "general" members and over 300,000 dues paying members. The Council lobbies for social security revision, a national health insurance program, higher health and safety standards in nursing homes, and adequate housing and jobs for the elderly.

National Council on the Aging, Inc. (NCOA)
1829 L Street NW
Washington, DC 20036

The NCOA is a nonprofit umbrella organization of individuals, voluntary agencies and associations, business organizations, and labor unions united by the principle that elders are entitled to lives of dignity, security, physical, mental and social well-being, and to full participation in society. NCOA works to make society more equitable for older persons, more caring and understanding of them so their rights are protected, and their needs are met in a humane, effective, and efficient manner.

National Institute on Aging (NIA)
9000 Rockville Pike
Bethesda, MD 20205

The NIA was established in 1974 for the conduct and support of biomedical, social and behavioral research and training related to the aging process and the diseases and other special problems and needs of elders. Thus it opposes ageism mainly through research and training to overcome stereotypes about aging and the aged.

National Senior Citizen's Law Center (NSCLC)
2025 M St. NW, Suite 400
Washington, DC 20036

The NSCLC is operated by a group of attorneys and is a nonprofit public interest organization that functions as an advocate for the elderly poor. Their specific functions include legal services, direct service provision, information dissemination, and education/training. They concentrate on opposing ageism directed against low-income elders.

Older Women's League (OWL)
730 Eleventh St. NW, Suite 300
Washington, DC 20001

OWL was founded in 1981 and now has more than 10,000 members and has chartered chapters in over 30 states. It is dedicated to advancing the interests of women in later life and to guaranteeing equality and quality of life for both sexes. Thus it combats both ageism and sexism.

Villers Advocacy Associates (VAA)
1334 G St. NW
Washington, DC 20005

VAA is an advocacy organization that seeks to foster through legislative means a movement of empowerment among elders, with particular emphasis on low-income elders. It is supported by the Villers Foundation (following).

The Villers Foundation, Inc.
1334 G. St. NW
Washington, DC 20005

This foundation was established in 1981 to foster fundamental changes in institutions and attitudes affecting elders. Seeking to nurture a movement of empowerment among elders, the foundation's main objectives are: to promote organizing and strengthening elder organizations that are sensitive to the needs of lower-income people; to help develop cooperation among elder groups; to help unite elders with their potential allies from intergenerational constituencies; to facilitate networking and innovations in the area of philanthropy to encourage greater support in the aging field; to support applied policy research and social change efforts; and to support media and public education around priority issues. They have an annual budget of up to $5 million.

SUMMARY

Most of the strategies that have been successful in reducing racism and sexism could be used to reduce ageism. Individual actions include informing yourself and others about aging, eliminating your own actions that express ageism, avoiding ageist language or jokes, writing letters to editors and officials, boycotting, and voting for candidates opposed to ageism.

Organized actions include gathering and disseminating information about aging, lobbying for legislation opposed to ageism, legal actions, grievance procedures, boycotts, rent strikes, watchdog activities, demonstrations, passive resistance and nonviolent confrontations, political campaigns, registering voters, and civil disobedience.

The major organizations working to reduce ageism include the Administration on Aging, the American Association of Retired Persons, the American Society on Aging, the Association for Gerontology in Higher Education, the Elvirita Lewis Foundation, the Gerontological Society of America, the Gray Panthers, the National Association for Hispanic Elderly, the National Caucus on Black Aged, the National Council of Senior Citizens, the National Council on the Aging, the National Institute on Aging, the Older Women's League, and the Villers Foundation.

We will conclude our book with a discussion of what the future of ageism may be.

15
The Future

There'll be love and laughter and peace ever after,
Tomorrow, just you wait and see.
                "The White Cliffs of Dover" (World War II song)

There is nothing certain but the unforeseen.
                                                    Ritter, 1976

HISTORICAL TRENDS

In this section we will consider whether the past trends that contributed to ageism will continue in the future and what that implies for the future of ageism.

In colonial times positive ageism was the rule, based on several factors: the relative scarcity of elders; the power of the family, the church, and tradition (all dominated by elders); elders' control of land and crafts; and elders as a major source of information.

These factors have all been reversed and show no sign of reverting to their status in colonial days. Elders are no longer scarce and their numbers will continue to increase for the foreseeable future. The family, the church, and tradition are no longer so powerful and they are less dominated by elders. There is little or no sign of reversals in these trends. Control of land and crafts is not so important in modern society and is becoming less important. Elders as a source of information have been eclipsed by books, magazines, television, and educational institutions.

Partly because of these trends, positive ageism has been greatly reduced and there is little prospect for a reemergence of positive ageism based on these factors. Furthermore, after the American Revolution, there was an accelerated emphasis on equality, individual achievement, secularism, and the free market. These ideologies also tended to undercut positive ageism.

Trends associated with modernization tended to encourage the growth of negative ageism after the Civil War. Demographic changes made the supply of older persons exceed the demand. The Industrial Revolution also decreased the demand for older persons. Rapidly changing technology tended to make the job skills of older workers obsolete.

However, two of the trends associated with modernization in the past may reverse themselves in the future. In the past, increased retirement lowered the income and social status of elders. Now retirement is becoming a more respected status and the disposable income and assets of retirees are often as high as or higher than they were before retirement (see Chapters 2 and 8). Similarly, in the past, urbanization often left elders behind in rural areas or deteriorated parts of the city. Now there are trends toward migration out of the central cities to suburban and semirural areas. Elders, with their greater assets and home equity, often join in (or lead) this migration pattern. Both of these reversals tend to undercut negative ageism.

Another reversal of a historical trend is the decrease in competition between older native workers and younger immigrant workers. This is much less intense now than it was around the turn of the century. In fact, there appear to be some growing labor shortages as the number of young workers entering the labor market declines, due to the coming of age of the "baby boom" generation. This trend may increase the demand for older workers to stay in the labor market or to reenter it on a part-time basis. This would tend to decrease discrimination against older workers.

CURRENT TRENDS

There are at least seven current trends that (if continued) will tend to reduce ageism in the future: the increasing knowledge and research about aging; the increasing health, education, and affluence of elders; the growing federal austerity; and the reductions in racism and sexism.

1. *Increasing knowledge about aging.* Knowledge about aging among the general public has not been measured until recently (Palmore, 1988). However, there is considerable evidence that interest in aging among the general public, the mass media, the government, and academia is increasing rapidly. Naisbitt (1982) found that space in the mass media devoted to aging increased rapidly during the 1970s. Legislation and programs for elders increased rapidly during the past 30 years. Courses on aging in colleges and universities multiplied during the past 20 years.

All of these trends increased general knowledge about aging and elders. This knowledge tends to reduce both positive and negative prejudice about elders.

2. *Growing scientific research on aging.* The Gerontological Society of America has grown from a few hundred members in the early 1960s to over 6,000 members in 1989. In the 1960s there were only two or three journals devoted to reporting gerontological research. Now there are over 40 professional journals in gerontology and several dozen books in the field published each year. Gerontological research has certainly been a growth industry during the past two decades.

This research has reduced ageism in two ways. First, it has revealed the true facts about aging, it has helped to distinguish between aging and disease, and in general has shown that normal aging is not as bad as the negative stereotypes portray it. Second, it has found ways to treat diseases common in old age, ways to prevent disease in old age, ways to slow the aging process, ways to extend longevity, and in general ways to improve the health and happiness of elders. This has tended to make the image of aging less negative.

3. *Improving health of elders.* Partly as a result of this research, partly as a result of better medical care through Medicare and Medicaid, partly as a result of healthier life-styles among elders, and partly as a result of the general improvement of health in our nation, elders as a group are getting healthier. Relative to the disabilities in the rest of the population, disabilities among those over 65 have been steadily declining at least since 1960 (Palmore, 1986).

This improving health and declining disability tends to undermine the stereotype that most elders are sick or disabled.

4. *Increasing education.* One of the most remarkable achievements of this century is the increase in literacy among elders from

a minority in 1900 to over 98 percent in 1979 (U.S. Bureau of the Census, 1984a). Similarly, educational attainment has increased rapidly: in 1959 persons over 65 had only three-fourths as many years of education as younger adults; but by the year 2000 they will have almost equal years of education (97%: U.S.Bureau of the Census, 1984a).

This trend is reducing ageism in several ways. It is reducing the generational education gap. It is challenging the stereotype of the illiterate or poorly educated elder. Perhaps most important, it contributes to more high level occupations and more affluence among elders.

5. *Increasing affluence.* Partly because of their increasing education, partly because of increasing programs to support elders, and partly because of the general increase in affluence, elders *as a group* have become more and more affluent each year. This affluence among elders is a dramatic change from the poverty so common during the 1930s. Before Social Security, poverty or financial dependence was the usual fate of a majority of elders. Even in 1980, there was still more poverty among elders than among others (Schick, 1986). But now there is less poverty among elders than among others, and elders receive a disproportionately larger share of the national personal income (Chapter 2).

This increasing affluence tends to undermine the stereotype of the pitiful elder depending on charity and handouts. Money talks in our society and this increasing affluence has made business listen to the interests and desires of elders, as well as increasing respect for elders in general.

6. *Growing federal austerity.* Since 1980, there have been more and more reductions in federal nondefense spending. So far, federal spending on most programs for elders have not been hard hit. But as the Gramm-Rudman Act forces ever greater cuts in federal programs, and as people realize that most elders are no longer poor, they may decide to reduce or eliminate some of the special programs and benefits for elders.

This would tend to reduce the positive ageism represented in such special programs. Of course there are other ways to balance the budget, such as deep cuts in military spending or large increases in taxes, but given prevailing sentiment against such alternatives, it seems more likely that cutting back on programs for elders will occur first, or at least in tandem with other alternatives.

7. *Declining racism and sexism.* While there have been ups and

downs in the struggle against various aspects of racism and sexism, most experts agree that there have been substantial reductions in both racism and sexism in our society during the past 50 years or so. These reductions may indirectly contribute to reductions in ageism in several ways.

First, people have become more aware of prejudice and discrimination in general and have become less likely to approve or practice it. Second, the legislation that was designed to reduce racism and sexism may also reduce ageism. Third, people working to reduce ageism can learn from the successes (and failures) of strategies to reduce racism and sexism. Finally, as racism and sexism wane, some people may turn more attention to reducing ageism because it is a relatively new and undeveloped concern.

Despite these positive trends, there is no quantitative evidence yet of actual reductions in ageism in our culture. The one analysis of recent trends as shown by two comparable surveys (1974–1981) found no decline in the general misperception that older people have more problems than they actually have (Ferraro, 1989).

ALTERNATE FUTURES

So far, the general trends outlined above seem to forecast reductions in ageism. However, there are some clouds on the horizon that may indicate some storms in the future.

Perhaps the most threatening cloud is the possibility of intergenerational conflict. We have concluded that such conflict is not likely in the immediate future (Chapter 5). But it is possible that some kind of backlash may develop from attempts to reduce negative ageism. Younger people may react by intensifying their prejudices and discriminations. Attempts to reduce positive ageism may go too far and tip the balance toward negative ageism. Elders may get defensive about their special privileges and benefits and attack anyone who would dare to question them.

Current special programs for elders will require a larger and larger portion of our government's budget unless they are reduced. Younger people may rebel against this growing burden and overreact by unfairly penalizing elders. Such conflict would encourage a rapid growth in ageism, both among younger people and among elders.

Another cloud is the possibility of a worldwide depression comparable to the great depression of the 1930s. Many economists have painted gloomy scenarios in which inflation becomes rampant on a worldwide basis, stock markets crash, banks and other investment institutions fail, and economies generally collapse. Such a catastrophe would mean the collapse of financial security for many or most elders. This might make the stereotype of the destitute elder a reality once more and encourage a resurgence of ageism.

A third cloud is the possibility of some terrible epidemic, such as AIDS, which would preoccupy our health care system to the extent that it could no longer care for elders the way it now does. Such a tragedy might result in age-based rationing of health care with elders getting much less because of their age.

A fourth cloud is formed by the ominous warnings about depletion of the ozone layer, the greenhouse effect, destruction of our rain forests, desertification, pollution of air and water, and so on. Such environmental disasters could preoccupy us and interfere with our attempts to reduce ageism. Elders might even be blamed for such problems because their generation's disregard for the environment would be a major cause of the problems.

Finally, the cloud that threatens the most devastation of all is the mushroom cloud: the proliferation of nuclear weapons both within the present nuclear club and by other nations who are developing nuclear weapons. If we have a nuclear war, there will be few elders (and few younger people) left and ageism will be of little concern to any survivor.

However, these are only clouds on the horizon at present and the most likely forecast seems to be "fair and mild."

FUTURE ROLE OF GERONTOLOGY

In his recent article calling for a new role for gerontology, Robert Morris (1989) made several recommendations that would tend to reduce ageism:

1. Devote more attention in agency operations and research to the positive side of aging to balance (not replace) the past emphasis on dependency, helplessness, deprivation, and cure of disease.
2. Broaden inquiry into future roles for those active retired who are interested, including both entrepreneurial and unpaid cooperative action.

3. Reverse the past tendency to move the elderly out of the mainstream of social and economic life and begin reintegrating.

4. Reintegrate the interests of the aged (and of their large infrastructure) with those of other age groups. Would it be committing an oxymoron to call for a nonageist policy on aging? By that, I mean to view the elderly as the spearhead or vanguard of renewed efforts to meet common human needs, rather than concentrating on the specialty needs of the aged.

I heartily concur with these recommendations.

SUMMARY

The factors that contributed to the positive ageism of colonial days have been reversed and are not likely to contribute to positive ageism in the future. Trends associated with modernization encouraged the growth of negative ageism after the Civil War: increasing numbers of elders, the industrial revolution, and rapidly changing technology.

Three trends of the past may reverse themselves and undercut negative ageism: decreased income and status due to retirement, isolation of elders due to urbanization, and competition between younger immigrant workers and older native workers.

Several current trends will continue to reduce ageism: increasing knowledge and research about aging; increasing health, education, and affluence of elders; growing federal austerity; and declining racism and sexism.

However, there are some threatening clouds on the horizon that could interfere with the reduction of ageism: intergenerational conflict, worldwide depression, epidemics, environmental disaster, and nuclear war. So far, these are only clouds and the most likely forecast seems to be "fair and mild."

Appendix A
The Facts on Aging Quizzes

These three Facts on Aging Quizzes are reprinted from Palmore, 1988. That book contains full documentation on the correct answers and instructions for various uses of the quizzes (Copyright is held by Springer Publishing Company). I suggest you try them out on yourself by marking each statement "T" for true, "F" for false, or "?" for don't know. Each quiz can be answered in about five minutes. The key to the correct answers may be found at the end of this appendix.

THE FACTS ON AGING QUIZ: PART 1 (FAQ1)

1. The majority of old people (age 65+) are senile (have defective memory, are disoriented, or demented).
2. The five senses (sight, hearing, taste, touch, and smell) all tend to weaken in old age.
3. The majority of old people have no interest in, nor capacity for, sexual relations.
4. Lung vital capacity tends to decline in old age.
5. The majority of old people feel miserable most of the time.
6. Physical strength tends to decline in old age.
7. More than one-tenth of the aged are living in long-stay institutions (such as nursing homes, mental hospitals, homes for the aged, etc.).

8. Aged drivers have fewer accidents per driver than those under age 65.
9. Older workers usually cannot work as effectively as younger workers.
10. Over three-fourths of the aged are healthy enough to carry out their normal activities.
11. The majority of old people are unable to adapt to change.
12. Old people usually take longer to learn something new.
13. It is difficult for the average old person to learn something new.
14. Older people tend to react slower than younger people.
15. In general, old people tend to be pretty much alike.
16. The majority of old people say they are seldom bored.
17. The majority of old people are socially isolated.
18. Older workers have fewer accidents than younger workers.
19. Over 15% of the population are now age 65 or over.
20. The majority of medical practitioners tend to give low priority to the aged.
21. The majority of old people have incomes below the poverty line (as defined by the federal government).
22. The majority of old people are working or would like to have some kind of work to do (including housework and volunteer work).
23. Old people tend to become more religious as they age.
24. The majority of old people say they are seldom irritated or angry.
25. The health and economic status of old people will be about the same or worse in the year 2000 (compared to younger people).

THE FACTS ON AGING QUIZ: PART 2 (FAQ2)

1. A person's height tends to decline in old age.
2 More older persons (65 or over) have chronic illnesses that limit their activity than do younger persons.
3 Older persons have more acute (short-term) illnesses than do younger persons.
4 Older persons have more injuries in the home than younger persons.
5 Older workers have less absenteeism than do younger workers.

6 Blacks' life expectancy at age 65 is about the same as whites'.
7 Men's life expectancy at age 65 is about the same as women's.
8 Medicare pays over half of the medical expenses for the aged.
9 Social Security benefits automatically increase with inflation.
10 Supplemental Security Income guarantees a minimum income for needy aged.
11 The aged do not get their proportionate share of the nation's income.
12 The aged have higher rates of criminal victimization than younger persons.
13 The aged are more fearful of crime than are younger persons.
14 The aged are the most law-abiding of all adult age groups.
15 There are about equal numbers of widows and widowers among the aged.
16 More of the aged vote than any other age group.
17 There are proportionately more older persons in public office than in the total population.
18 The proportion of Blacks among the aged is growing.
19 Participation in voluntary organizations (churches and clubs) tends to decline among the healthy aged.
20 The majority of old people live alone.
21 The aged have a lower rate of poverty than the rest of the population.
22 The rate of poverty among aged Blacks is about three times as high as among aged whites.
23 Older persons who reduce their activity tend to be happier than those who do not.
24 When the last child leaves home, the majority of parents have serious problems adjusting to their "empty nest."
25 The proportion of widowed among the aged is decreasing.

THE FACTS ON AGING AND MENTAL HEALTH QUIZ (FAMHQ)

1. The majority of persons over 65 have some mental illness severe enough to impair their normal abilities.
2. Cognitive impairment (memory loss, disorientation, or confusion) is an inevitable part of old age.

3. If an older mental patient makes up false stories, it is best to point out that he or she is lying, in order to reduce this behavior.
4. The prevalence of neurosis and schizophrenia increases in old age.
5. Suicide rates increase with age for women past 45.
6. Suicide rates increase with age for men past 45.
7. Fewer of the aged have mental illnesses, when all types are added together, than do other age groups.
8. The primary mental health problem of old age is cognitive impairment.
9. Alzheimer's disease (progressive senile dementia) is the most common type of chronic cognitive impairment among the aged.
10. There is no cure for Alzheimer's disease.
11. Most patients with Alzheimer's disease act the same way.
12. Organic brain impairment is easy to distinguish from functional mental illness.
13. It is best not to look directly at older mental patients when you are talking to them.
14. It is best to avoid talking to demented patients because it may increase their confusion.
15. Demented patients should not be allowed to talk about their past, because it may depress them.
16. The prevalence of cognitive impairment increases in old age.
17. Isolation and hearing loss are the most frequent causes of paranoid disorders in old age.
18. Poor nutrition may produce mental illness among the elderly.
19. Mental illness is more prevalent among the elderly with less income and education.
20. The majority of nursing home patients suffer from mental illness.
21. The elderly have less sleep problems than younger persons.
22. Major depression is more prevalent among the elderly than among younger persons.
23. Widowhood is more stressful for older women than for younger women.
24. More of the aged use mental health services than do younger persons.
25. Psychotherapy is usually ineffective with older patients.

KEY TO CORRECT ANSWERS

FAQ1: All the odd numbered items are false and all the even numbered are true.

FAQ2: Alternating pairs of items are true or false; that is, 1 and 2 are true, 3 and 4 are false, 5 and 6 are true, and so forth, and 25 is true.

FAMHQ: Alternating sets of five items are false or true; that is the first five items are false; the next five (6–10) are true; the next five (11–15) are false; the next five (16–20) are true; and the last five (21–25) are false.

Appendix B
Ageist Humor

The following jokes are classified first into two major sections: Negative and Positive. Within each section the humor is listed alphabetically by topic. Most of this humor is anonymous. The author or source is cited when it is known. The jokes are often embellished with more detail than is given here. These jokes are written to bring out their ageist aspects.

NEGATIVE HUMOR

Activity

You've reached old age when all you exercise is caution.

"There isn't a single thing I can't do now that I could do at 18—which gives you an idea of how pathetic I was at 18!"
George Burns

"There's a similarity between babies and old men—both fall asleep over their bottles."
Earl Wilson

Age Concealment

The age of some old folks is like the speedometer on a used car— you know it's been set back but you don't know how far.

Aging (general)

Old age is the time of life when one regards the rising generation as a falling one.

A "mature adult" is one who has stopped belonging to the younger generation and started criticizing it.

"We do not count a man's years until he has nothing else to count."
Ralph Waldo Emerson

Just when you make it over the hump, you find that you're over the hill.

Aging is a process in which man loses his hair, his illusions, and what little patience he may have had.

Appearance

"Old Age: when the mind forgets—and the mirror reminds."
Pat Weber

Time may be a great healer, but he certainly is no beauty specialist.

First man: "Did you see the pleased expression on the face of that woman when I told her that she didn't look a day older than her daughter?"
Second man: "No, I was too busy looking at the expression on the face of her daughter."

An old lady in a nursing home decided to streak down the hall and through the dining room.
One man askes another, "What did she have on?"
Answer, "I don't know, but whatever it was, it sure was wrinkled."

An old man attending a flower exhibition, took off all his clothes and streaked from one end of the hall to the other. He was awarded a blue ribbon for "Best Dried Arrangement."

Birthday Cards

(*On front:*) The trouble with being our age, by the time our ship comes in,
(*Inside:*) our piers have collapsed.

(*On front:*) You can do everything a 21-year-old can,
(*Inside:*) Only not so often.

(On front:) Don't just sit there. If someone calls you old,
(*Inside:*) Run them over with your wheelchair.

(*On front:*) You know you're aging when you have a hangover . . .
(*Inside:*) and had nothing to drink.

(*On front:*) You don't have to worry about your age.
(*Inside:*) You should, but you don't have to.

(*On front:*) I know you're going to have a lot of good clean fun on
your birthday . . .
(*Inside:*) Because you're too old to swing.

Longevity

The secret of living to be 100 becomes less attractive as you get
older.

A host greets an 80-year-old visitor: "We're glad to have you here."
"At my age I'm glad to be anywhere," he responded.

Old-Fashioned

At a certain age some people's minds close up; they live on intellectual fat.

Reporter: "How long have you lived around here?"
Old man: "Eighty-five years."
Reporter: "You've seen a lot of changes, haven't you?"
Old man: "Yep, and I've been ag'in all of 'em!"

Marriage

An old woman met an old man and asked him why he looked so
pale. "Well, I've been in jail for the last ten years."
"Why?"
"Well, I murdered my wife."
"Oh, so you're single, eh?"

An old woman met an old man and said, "You remind me of
somebody"
"Who?"
"My third husband."
"Your third husband! How many husbands have you had?"
"Two."

Mental Impairment

A gerontologist was lecturing about aging processes: "There are three signs of aging: First, there is loss of memory . . . (pause) and I've forgotten the other two."

Three elders were talking about their memory problems. First one says, "I keep forgetting to take my keys with me and I get locked out of my house or car."
Second one says, "I have a terrible time remembering people's names.
Third one says, "My memory's been pretty good lately, knock on wood." He then knocks on wood and immediately turns and calls out, "Hello? Who's that knocking?"

An 82-year-old man was being kidded by the younger fellows about his continuing potency. But he just shook his head and said, "It ain't no fun to be old, because your memory goes bad on you. . . . Why just the other night I woke up with an erection, so I roused my wife to have a little fun. But she says for me to shut up because we have already done it twice that night. It's kind of sad when a man gets so old he can't remember things like that."

An old golfer was complaining that he couldn't play golf anymore because he could no longer see the ball after he had hit it. His friend volunteered to watch the ball for him because, he said, "I have the eyes of an eagle." So the next day the old golfer teed off and asked his friend, "Did you see it?"
"Of course," came the reply, "I have the eyes of an eagle."
"Well, where did it go?"
"I forgot."

A minister was visiting an elder in a nursing home. He noticed a bowl of peanuts on the bedside table and helped himself to some as he talked to his parishioner. When he was leaving he said, "Thanks for the peanuts."
"You're quite welcome. With my teeth so bad these days, it's all I can do to suck the chocolate off them."

Old man losing his memory, gets memory pills from his doctor.
Friend: "How do they work?"
Old man: "Fine, only I forget to take them."

Physical Impairment

Careful grooming may make you look 20 years younger, but it won't fool a flight of stairs.

Old age is an incurable disease.

Plaque on a kitchen wall: "Don't criticize the coffee. Remember you too will be weak one of these days!"

Old man and woman are sitting on a park bench. He says, "I have two questions: Will you marry me, and will you help me up off this bench?"

You're getting old when it takes longer to rest than to get tired.

Elderly man to daughter, "Doc said to exercise—I think I'll start riding a bike again."
Daughter: "That'd be good for you daddy. They've got nice 3-wheelers you can get."

The five "B"'s of aging are: baldness, bridgework, bifocal, bulges, and bunions.

"Old age is when your legs buckle and your belt doesn't."
Earl Wilson

"There are some advantages being my age. For example, you can't get any more illness: you've had them all."
George Burns

By the time a man gets to greener pastures, he can't climb the fence.

Elderly man to travel agent: "Never mind the water skiing—how about the deck chairs?"

You're old when you exchange emotions for symptoms.
It's not that we're more agreeable as the keen eyesight of youth passes; all that nodding up and down is adjusting the bifocal glasses.

Sexuality

An elderly couple had a ritual of touching hands each night in bed before going to sleep. One night the husband did not reach over to touch hands. The wife asked, "Aren't we going to touch hands tonight?"
"Not tonight, dear, I'm too tired," he replied.

A 75 year-old man dates a young girl and they start necking. They neck and neck a long time. Finally, the young girl says, "Old man, you've had it." He says with surprise, "I have?"

"Did you hear that our 82-year-old neighbor married a 19-year-old girl?
"No fooling?"
"Well, very little."

King David and King Solomon lived merry, merry lives;
With many, many lady friends and many, many wives.
But when old age crept onward with all its many qualms,
King Solomon wrote Proverbs and King David wrote the Psalms.

"Young men want to be faithful and are not; old men want to be faithless and cannot."

Oscar Wilde

You're getting old when your wife gives up sex for Lent and you don't even notice it.

Old man: "Why don't you tell me when you're having an orgasm?"
Wife: "I would, but you're never there."

A 55-year-old man told his wife that he qualified for Social Security benefits by unbuttoning his shirt and showing the gray hair on his chest.
Wife: "Too bad you didn't unzip your fly; you could have qualified for disability benefits too."

An old man was complaining to his wife: "Sometimes when we make love I feel hot, and sometimes I feel cold."
Wife: "That's because we make love only twice a year: once in the summer and once in the winter!"

Urinary Problems

Little boy went to the men's room by himself and stayed a long time. After a while he came out crying because he had wet his pants. His father asked him what had happened. "Well, there were only two urinals and there were two old men at them. One old man couldn't start. The other old man couldn't stop. And I couldn't wait."

An elder ordered a scotch and water with one shot of scotch and four shots of water. He drank that down and then ordered one with two shots of scotch and two shots of water. He drank that down and then ordered one with straight scotch. The bartender asked him why. "At my age you can hold your scotch better than you can hold your water."

POSITIVE HUMOR

Aging (General)

At 10, a child; at 20, wild; at 30, tame if ever; at 40, wise; at 50, rich; at 60, good, or never.

> *"To be 70 years young is sometimes far more cheerful and hopeful than to be 40 years young."*
> Oliver Wendel Holmes

> *"To grow old is to pass from passion to compassion."*
> Albert Camus

Worship age and you'll look forward to life. Worship youth and you'll create your own obsolescence.

Birthday Cards

(*On front:*) Dearie, you may be getting to be an oldie . . .
(*Inside:*) But you'll always be a goodie.

(*On front:*) You're only as old as you feel . . .
(*Inside:*) And last night when I felt you, you felt as young as ever!

(*On front:*) Nobody should call you an old codger;
(*Inside:*) A **sexy** old codger would be more accurate.

Cleverness

An old rabbi and a young rabbi were candidates for village rabbi. They were put up overnight in adjacent rooms with rather thin walls. The old rabbi was worried and practiced his speech over and over again for several hours. The next day the young rabbi goes first and gives the speech of the old rabbi, which he has memorized from listening through the wall. The old rabbi then says, "I had a speech prepared, but since my younger colleague has given such a brilliant speech, I will simply show you how clever I am by repeating his speech word for word," which he did and won the appointment.

Finances

Old Timer: a fellow who has made the last payment on his house.

Longevity

An anthropologist visiting in Soviet Georgia was impressed by an old man carrying a big load of bricks. He asked how old the man was. The reply was, "About 80, but we have more remarkable men than that." Soon they came upon another old man carrying an even bigger load of bricks. "How old is he?"
"About 90, but we have more remarkable men than that." Then a third old man vaulted over a fence and ran up the street. "How old is he and why is he running?"
"He's about 100, and he's running home to make love to his wife for the third time today—you see she's losing her memory."

Reporter: "How does it feel to be 90 years old?"
Man: "Wonderful. Not an enemy in the world!"
Reporter: "What a beautiful thought!"
Man: "Yep, I've outlived them all!"

A reporter was interviewing a man on his 100th birthday: "Have you lived here all your life?"
"Not yet!"

"Don't you hate to be as old as 95?"
"Nope. If I wasn't this old, I'd be dead."

When the reporter asked a man on his 100th birthday if he had any sons, he replied, "Not yet!"

Reporter to a man on his 99th birthday: "I hope I can see you again next year."
"Well, son, I expect you will; you look healthy enough to me!"

A doctor examining an 80-year-old patient found him in excellent health. The doctor asked,
"How old was your father when he died?"
"He's still living and he's 100 years old."
"Really? Where is he? I'd like to examine him."
"He's attending the wedding of *his* father who is 120!"
"Really? Isn't that silly for a 120-year-old man to remarry?"
"Well, maybe, but you see, he made the girl pregnant so he has to marry her."

George Bernard Shaw found a tombstone in a village that said, "Died at age 86. Cut down in the prime of life. "He decided that was where he wanted to retire.

Old Maids

An old maid is a woman who has missed the opportunity of getting divorced.

Retirement

Man who has retired after 40 years of rushing to catch the commuter train, to his wife: Please turn my eggs over this morning; I don't like them sunny side up."
"Why didn't you ever say so before?"
"I didn't have time before."

Sexuality

A group of women are discussing how late in life a woman loses her sexual appetite. They ask an 80-year-old grandmother who says, "Sorry, girls, you'll have to ask somebody older than me."

"Did you hear Reggie was named in a paternity suit?"
"Is that right? Why, he must be 75 years old!"
"Right, and now he's so proud, he won't hardly talk to you!"

Old lady to friend: "I had a lot of trouble last night. A man kept banging on my door."
"Why didn't you open it?"
"What and let him out?"

Doctor tells a 70-year-old patient that she is pregnant. She calls her 80-year-old husband and says, "Honey, I'm pregnant!" Husband (cautiously), "Who is this calling?"

"A man is only as old as the woman he feels."
                                                                                     Groucho Marx

A 75-year-old woman asked her doctor for a complete physical examination because something was wrong. Her gave her an examination and found nothing wrong. He asked her, "What seem to be your symptoms?"
"I seem to be losing my sexual desire."

"Well, that's not unusual for a woman your age. When did you first notice it?"
"I noticed it last night and then again this morning!"

An old man approached his doctor and said, "Doctor, I'm slowly going nuts over women. Is there any way to speed it up?"

A 90-year-old groom was recounting his new wedding: "The first evening two of my sons carried me up the stairs to our nuptial suite, and the next morning it took four of them to bring me down to breakfast."
"Why did it take four sons to bring you downstairs?"
"I fought 'em!"

Three old men were discussing who they would like to be buried next to. The first man said Washington, the second man said Socrates, and the third said Dolly Parton. The first man objected: "But she's not dead yet."
Third man: "I know. Neither am I!"

Wisdom

At age 20 we don't care what the world thinks of us; at 40 we worry about what the world thinks of us; at 60 we discover it wasn't thinking of us at all!

A wise old owl sat on an oak.
The more he saw the less he spoke;
The less he spoke the more he heard.
Why can't we be like that wise old bird?"

                                                          Edward Hersey Richards

References

Achenbaum, W. (1978). *Old age in a new land.* Baltimore, MD: Johns Hopkins University Press.

Achenbaum, W., & Kusnerz, E. (1978). *Images of old age.* Ann Arbor, MI: Institute of Gerontology.

Adorno, T., Frenel-Brunswick, E., Levinson, D., & Sanford, R. (1950). *The authoritarian personality.* New York: Harper & Row.

Ansello, E. (1977). Age and ageism in children's first literature. *Educational Gerontology, 2,* 211.

Ansello, E. (1978). The older woman in television. Paper presented at the meeting of the Gerontological Society of America. Dallas, TX.

Arluke, A., Levine, J., & Suchwalko, J. (1984). Sexuality and romance in advice books for the elderly. *Gerontologist, 24,* 415.

Aronoff, C. (1974). Old age in prime time. *Journal of Communication, 24,* 86.

Atchley, R. (1982). Retirement as a social institution. *Annual Review of Sociology, 8,* 263.

Atchley, R. (1987a). Age grading and grouping. In G. Maddox (Ed.), *The encyclopedia of aging.* New York: Springer Publishing Co.

Atchley, R. (1987b). Political behavior. In G. Maddox (Ed.), *The encyclopedia of aging.* New York: Springer Publishing Co.

Atchley, R. (1988). *Social forces and aging.* Belmont, CA: Wadsworth.

Austin, D. (1985). Attitudes toward old age. *Gerontologist, 25,* 431.

Axelrod, S., & Eisdorfer, C. (1961). Attitudes toward old people. *Journal of Gerontology, 16,* 75.

Back, K. (1987). Age norms. In G. Maddox (Ed.), *The encyclopedia of aging.* New York: Springer Publishing Co.

Baird, M. (1986). *The birds of sadness.* New York: St Martin's Press.

Barbato, C., & Feezel, J. (1987). The language of aging in different age groups. *Gerontologist, 27,* 527.

Barron, M. (1961). *The Aging American.* New York: Crowell.

Barrow, G., & Smith, P. (1979). *Aging, ageism, and society.* St. Paul, MN: West Publishing Co.

Beaver, M. (1983). *Human service practice with the elderly.* Englewood Cliffs, NJ: Prentice Hall.

Bentson, L. (1988). Interveiw on television, August 16, 1988.

Berelson, B., & Steiner, G. (1964). *Human behavior.* New York: Harcourt, Brace.

Binstock, R. (1972). Interest group liberalism and the politics of aging. *Gerontologist, 12,* 265.

Binstock, R. (1983). The aged as scapegoat. *Gerontologist, 23,* 136.

Binstock, R. (1987). Health care: Organization, use, and financing. In G. Maddox (Ed.), *The encyclopedia of aging.* New York: Springer Publishing Co.

Blazer, D. (1980). The epidemiology of mental illness in late life. In E. Busse & D. Blazer (Eds.), *Handbook of geriatric psychiatry.* New York: Van Nostrand Reinhold.

Blazer, D., & Pennybacker, M. (1984). Epidemiology of alcoholism in the elderly. In T. Hartford & T. Samorajiski (Eds.), *Alcoholism in the elderly.* New York: Raven.

Borgatta, E. (1987). Filial responsibility. In G. Maddox (Ed.), *The encyclopedia of aging.* New York: Springer Publishing Co.

Botwinick, J. (1967). *Cognitive processes in maturity and old age.* New York: Springer Publishing Co.

Braithwaite, V. (1986). Old age stereotypes. *Journal of Gerontology, 41,* 353.

Breen, L. (1960). The aging individual. In C. Tibbit (Ed.), *Handbook of social gerontology,* Chicago: The Univeristy of Chicago Press.

Broom, L., & Selznick, P. (1968). *Sociology* (Fourth Edition). New York: Harper & Row.

Bultena, G., & Wood, V. (1969). The American retirement community. *Journal of Gerontology, 24,* 209.

Bunzel, J. (1972). Note on the history of a concept—Gerontophobia. *Gerontologist, 12,* 116.

Burgess, E. (Ed.) (1960). *Aging in western societies.* Chicago: University of Chicago Press.

Busse, E., & Blazer, D. (Eds.). (1980). *Handbook of geriatric psychiatry.* New York: Van Nostrand Reinhold.

Butler, R. (1969). Ageism: Another form of bigotry. *Gerontologist, 9,* 243.

Butler, R. (1975). *Why survive: Being old in America.* New York: Harper & Row.

Butler, R. (1987). Ageism. In G. Maddox (Ed.), *The encyclopedia of aging.* New York: Springer Publishing Co.

Butler, R. (1987a). Geriatrics. In G. Maddox (Ed.), *The encyclopedia of aging.* New York: Springer Publishing Co.

Butler, R., & Lewis, M. (1982). *Aging and mental health.* St. Louis, MO: Mosby Co.

Callahan, D. (1987). *Setting limits*. New York: Simon & Schuster.

Cameron, P. (1970). The generation gap: Beliefs about sexuality and self-reported sexuality. *Developmental Psychology, 3*, 272.

Campbell, J., & Strate, J. (1981). Are old people conservative? *Gerontologist, 21*, 580.

Carp, F. (1975). Life-style and location within the city. *Gerontologist, 15*, 27.

Carr, C. (1982). Giving the hospitalized elderly the best nursing care possible. *Health Services Manager, 15*, 6.

Chaneles, S. (1987). Growing old behind bars. *Psychology Today* (October), 48.

Chen, Y. (1988). Making assets out of tomorrow's elders. In R. Morris & S. Bass (Eds.), *Retirement reconsidered*. New York: Springer Publishing Co.

Christie, R., & Cook, P. (1958). A guide to published literature relating to the authoritarian personality. *Journal of Psychology* (April), 171.

Clark, M. (1980). The poetry of aging. *Gerontologist, 20*, 188.

Clark, R. (1987). Economics. In G. Maddox (Ed.), *The encyclopedia on aging*. New York: Springer Publishing Co.

Clark, R., Maddox, G., Schrimper, R., & Sumner, D. (1984). *Inflation and the economic well-being of the elderly*. Baltimore, MD: The Johns Hopkins University Press.

Clayton, V. (1987). Wisdom. In G. Maddox (Ed.), *The encyclopedia of aging*. New York: Springer Publishing Co.

Cohen, E. (1988). The elderly mystique: Constraints on the autonomy of the elderly with disabilities. *Gerontologist, 28*, 24.

Cohen, E., & Kruschwitz, A. (1990). Old age in America represented in 19th and 20th century sheet music. *Gerontologist, 30*, 345.

Cohen, G. (1987). Alzheimer's Disease. In G. Maddox (Ed.), *The encyclopedia of aging*. New York: Springer Publishing Co.

Cohen, R. (1989). Age before beauty. *Washington Post Magazine*, December 17, p. 11.

Covey, H. (1988). Historical terminology used to represent older people. *Gerontologist, 28*, 291.

Covey, H. (1989). Perceptions and attitudes toward sexuality of the elderly during the Middle Ages. *Gerontologist, 29*, 93.

Cowgill, D. (1974). Aging and modernization. In J. Gubrium (Ed.), *Late life, communities, and environmental policy*. Springfield, IL: Thomas.

Craft, J., Doctors, S., Shkop, Y, & Benecki, T. (1979). Simulated management perceptions, hiring decisions and age. *Aging and Work* (Spring), 95.

Crawford, T. (1974). Sermons on racial tolerance and the parish neighborhood context. *Journal of Applied Social Psychology, 4*, 1.

Crease, R. (1987). None but the bald. *50 Plus*, (February), 74.

Crimmins, E., Saito, Y., & Ingegneri, D. (1989). Changes in life expectancy and disability-free life expectancy in the United States. *Population and Development Review, 15*, 235.

Cryns, A., & Monk, A. (1972). Attitudes of the aged toward the young. *Journal of Gerontology*, *27*, 107.

Crystal, S. (1982). *America's old age crisis*. New York: Basic Books.

Cutler, S. (1973). Perceived prestige loss and political attitudes among the aged. *Gerontologist*, *13*, 69.

Cutler, S. (1987). Crime. In G. Maddox (Ed.), *The encyclopedia of aging*. New York: Springer Publishing Co.

Cumming, E., & Henry, E. (1961). *Growing old*. New York: Basic Books.

Davies, L. (1977). Attitudes toward old age and aging as shown by humor. *Gerontologist*, *18*, 76.

Davis, R. (1987). Images of aging in the media. In G. Maddox (Eds), *Encyclopedia of aging*. New York: Springer Publishing Co.

Davis, R., & Davis, J. (1985). *TV's image of the elderly*. Lexington, MA: Lexington Books.

Demos, V., & Jache, A. (1981 September 22). Return to sender—please! *Women's Day*, 20.

Dillon, K., & Jones, R. (1981). Attitudes toward aging portrayed by birthday cards. *International Journal of Aging and Human Development*, *13*, 79.

Doering, M., Rhodes, S., & Schuster, M. (1983). *The aging worker*. Beverly Hills, CA: Sage.

Dowd, J., & Bengtson, V. (1978) Aging in minority populations. *Journal of Gerontology*, *33*, 427.

Drevenstedt, J. (1976). Perceptions of onsets of young adulthood, middle age, and old age. *Journal of Gerontology*, *31*, 53.

Eisele, F. (1987). Gerontocracy. In G. Maddox (Ed.), *The encyclopedia of aging*. New York: Springer Publishing Co.

Elliott, J. (1984). The daytime television drama portrayal of older adults. *Gerontologist*, *24*, 628.

Erikson, E. (1968). Life cycle. In *International encyclopedia of the social sciences*. NY: Macmillan.

Estes, C. (1979). *The aging enterprise*. San Francisco: Jossey-Bass.

Estes, C. (1983). *Long-term care: need for a national policy*. U.S. House Select Committee on Aging. Dec. 15, 1983. Hearing Transcript.

Estes, C., & Binney, E. (1989). The biomedicalization of aging. *Gerontologist*, *29*, 587.

Federal Bureau of Investigation. (1981). *Uniform crime reports*. Washington, DC: U.S. Government Printing Office.

Ferraro, K. (1989). Self and older person referents in evaluating life problems, 1974–1981. *Gerontologist*, *29*, (October special issue) 231A.

Finch, C., & Haylflick, L. (Eds.). (1977). *Handbook of the biology of aging*. New York: Van Nostrand Reinhold.

Fischer, D. (1978). *Growing old in America*. New York: Oxford University Press.

Foner, A. (1987). Age conflicts. In G. Maddox (Ed.), *The encyclopedia of aging*. New York: Springer Publishing Co.

Frankfather, D. (1977). *The aged in the community.* New York: Praeger.

Fredrickson, B., Collins, C., and Carstensen, L. (1989). Affective interpretations of old and young neutral faces. *Gerontologist, 29,* (October special issue) 231A.

Fried, E., Rivlin, A., Schultze, C., and Teeters, N. (1973). *Setting national priorities.* Washington, DC: Brookings Institute.

Friedan, B. (1963). *The feminine mystique.* New York: Norton.

Gaitz, C., & Baer, P. (1971). Characteristics of elderly patients with alcoholism. *Archives of General Psychiatry, 24,* 372.

Gelwicks, L. (1987). Achitecture. In G. Maddox (Ed.), *The encyclopedia of aging.* New York: Springer Publishing Co.

Gelwicks, L., & Newcomer, R. (1974). *Planning housing environments for the elderly.* Washington, DC: National Council on the Aging.

George, L. (1984). The institutionalized. In E. Palmore (Ed.), *Handbook on the aged in the United States.* Westport, CT: Greenwood Press.

George, L. (1985). Socialization to old age. In E. Palmore (ed.) *Normal aging III.* Durham, NC: Duke University Press.

Gerbner, G., Grass, L., Signorielli, N., & Morgan, M. (1980). Aging with television. *Journal of Communication, 30,* 2.

Glenn, N., & Grimes, M. (1968). Aging, voting, and political interest. *American Sociological Review, 33,* 563.

Golant, S. (1975). Residential concentrations of the future elderly. *Gerontologist, 15,* 16.

Golde, P., & Kogan, N. (1959). A sentence completion procedure for assessing attitudes toward old people. *Journal of Gerontology, 14,* 355.

Gulliver, P. (1968). Age differentiation. *International encyclopedia of social science.* New York: Macmillan.

Haber, P. (1987). Hospice. In G. Maddox (Ed.), *Encyclopedia of Aging.* New York: Springer Publishing Co.

Hagestad, G., & Neugarten, B. (1985). Age and the life course. In R. Binstock & E. Shanas (Eds.), *Handbook of aging and the social sciences.* New York: Van Nostrand Reinhold.

Hamilton, D. (1981). *Cognitive processes in stereotyping and intergroup behavior.* Hillsdale, NJ: Lawrence Erlbaum.

Harris, A., & Feinberg, J. (1977). Television and aging. *Gerontologist, 17,* 464.

Harris, L. (1975). *The myth and reality of aging in America.* Washington, DC: The National Council on the Aging.

Harris, L. (1981). *Aging in the eighties: America in transition.* Washington, DC: The National Council on the Aging.

Havighurst, R. (1968). Personality and patterns of aging. *Gerontologist, 8,* 20.

Hickey, T., & Douglass, R. (1981). Neglect and abuse of older family members. *Gerontologist, 21,* 171.

Hickey, T., Hickey, L., & Kalish, R. (1968). Children's perception of the elderly. *Journal of Genetic Psychology, 112*, 227.

Hickey, T., & Kalish, R. (1968). Young people's perception of adults. *Journal of Gerontolgy, 23*, 215.

Hodge, M. (1987). Why women lie about their age. *50 Plus* (February), 40.

Hudson, R. (1987). Federal budgeting and expenditures. In G. Maddox, (Ed.), *The encyclopedia of aging*. New York: Springer Publishing Co.

Hudson, R., & Strate, J. (1985). Aging and political systems. In R. Binstock, & E. Shanas, (Eds.), *Handbook on aging and the social sciences*. New York: Van Nostrand Reinhold.

Inciardi, J., McBride, D., Russe, B., & Wells, K. (1978). Acute drug reactions among the aged. *Addictive Diseases, 3*, 383.

Jacobs, J. (1974). *Fun city*. New York: Holt, Rinehart, and Winston.

Jacobs, R., & Vinick, B. (1977). *Re-engagement in later life*. Stamford, CT: Greylock.

Jantz, R., Seefeldt, C., Cunningham, J., & Serock, K. (1978). *Children's attitudes toward the elderly*. Unpublished report. University of Maryland.

Kahana, B. (1987). Isolation. In G. Maddox (Ed.), *The encyclopedia of aging*. New York: Springer Publishing Co.

Kahana, E., & Kahana, B. (1985). Jews. In E. Palmore (Ed.), *Handbook on the aged in the United States*. Westport, CT: Greenwood Press.

Kalish, R. (1979). The new ageism and the failure models. *Gerontologist, 19*, 398.

Karp, D. (1988). A decade of reminders: Changing age consciousness between 50 and 60 years old. *Gerontologist, 28*, 727.

Kart, C., Metress, E., & Metress, S. (1988). *Aging, health, and society*. Boston: Jones & Bartlett.

Kastenbaum, R. (1987a). Suicide. In G. Maddox (Ed.), *The encyclopedia of aging*. New York: Springer Publishing Co.

Kastenbaum, R. (1987b). Life-Course. In G. Maddox (Ed.), *The encyclopedia of aging*. New York: Springer Publishing Co.

Kausler, D. (1987). Memory and memory theory. In G. Maddox (Ed.), *The encyclopedia of aging*. New York: Springer Publishing Co.

Kearl, M. (1982). An inquiry into the positive personal and social effects of old age stereotypes among the elderly. *International Journal of Aging and Human Development, 14*, 277.

Kingson, E., Hirshorn, B., & Cornman, J. (1986). *Ties that bind: The interdependence of generations*. Cabin John, MD: Seven Locks Press.

Knowles, D. (1984). Middle-aged and older workers. In L. Yolles et al. (Eds.), *The aging employee*. New York: Human Sciences Press.

Kogan, N. (1973). Attitudes toward old people. *Journal of Abnormal and Social Psychology, 62*, 44.

Kolberg, L. (1973). Continuities in childhood and adult moral development revisited. In P. Baltes & K. Schaie (eds.), *Life-span developmental psychology*. New York: Academic Press.

Konner, M. (1988). Mortality. *New York Times Magazine* (December 4), 100.

Krauss, I. (1987a). Reaction time. In G. Maddox (Ed.), *The encyclopedia of aging.* New York: Springer Publishing Co.

Krauss, I. (1987b). Employment. In G. Maddox (Ed.), *The encyclopedia of aging.* New York: Springer Publishing Co.

Kutza, E. (1981). *The benefits of old age: Social welfare policy for the elderly.* Chicago: University of Chicago Press.

LaBouvie-Vief, G. (1985). Intelligence and cognition. In J. Birren & K. Schaie (Eds.), *Handbook of the psychology of aging.* (2nd ed.) New York: Van Nostrand Reinhold.

Laird, C. (1985). *Webster's new world thesaurus.* New York: Prentice Hall.

Lammers, W. (1987). Government programs: State. In G. Maddox (Ed.), *The encyclopedia of aging.* New York: Springer Publishing Co.

Larson, R. (1978). Thirty years of research on the subjective well-being of older Americans. *Journal of Gerontology, 40,* 109.

Laurie, W. (1987). Federal expenditures, Year 2000. In G. Maddox (Ed.), *The encyclopedia of aging.* New York: Springer Publishing Co.

Lawton, M. (1980). *Environment and aging.* Belmont, CA: Wadsworth.

Lebowitz, B. (1987). Mental health services. In G. Maddox (Ed.), *The encyclopedia of aging.* New York: Springer Publishing Co.

Lenski, G. (1966). *Power and Privilege.* New York: McGraw-Hill.

Lerner, M. (1957). *America as a civilization.* New York: Simon & Schuster.

Levin, J., & Levin, W. (1980). *Ageism: Prejudice and discrimination against the elderly.* Belmont, CA: Wadsworth.

Levin, J., & Levin, W. (1982). *The functions of discrimination and prejudice.* New York: Harper & Row.

Lobsenz, N. (1974). Sex and the senior citizen. *New York Times Magazine* (January 20), 8.

Longino, C. (1987). Subcultures. In G. Maddox (Ed.), *The encyclopedia of aging.* New York: Springer Publishing Co.

Longino, C. (1988). The gray peril mentality and the impact of retirement migration. *The Journal of Applied Gerontology, 7,* 448.

Longino, C., McClelland, K., & Peterson, W. (1980). The aged subculture hypothesis. *Journal of Gerontology, 35,* 758.

Loughman, C. (1980). Eros and the elderly: A literary view. *Gerontologist, 20,* 182.

Lubomudrov, S. (1987). Congressional perceptions of the elderly. *Gerontologist, 27,* 77.

Maddox, G., Abolafia, J., & Glass, T. (1985). Paying for health care: Experience of older adults in the 1970's. Paper presented at the 38th Annual Meeting of the Gerontological Society of America, New Orleans, LA, November 24.

Maddox, G., & Douglas, E. (1985). Aging and individual differences. In

Palmore, E. et al. (Eds.), *Normal aging III*. Durham, NC: Duke University Press.

Markides, K. (1983). Minority aging. In B. Riley, B. Hess, & K. Bond (Eds.), *Aging in society*. Hillsdale, NJ: Erlbaum.

Markides, K. (1987). Minorities and aging. In G. Maddox (Ed.), *The encyclopedia of aging*. New York: Springer Publishing Co.

Markson, E., Levitz, G., & Gognalons-Caillard, M. (1973). The elderly and the community. *Journal of Gerontology, 28*, 503.

Marotta, J., & Marotta, G. (1989). Shame on the Whoopies. *Washington Post*. August 8.

Masters, W., & Johnson, V. (1966). *Human sexual response*. Boston: Little, Brown & Co., Inc.

May, W. (1982). Who cares for the elderly? *The Hastings Center Report* (December).

McFarland, R. (1973). The need for functional age measurements in industrial gerontology. *Industrial Gerontology, 19*, 1.

McKee, P., & Kauppinen, H. (1987). *The art of aging*. New York: Human Sciences Press.

McTavish, D. (1971). Perceptions of old people: a review of research, methodologies, and findings. *Gerontolgist, 11*(No. 4, Pt. II), 90.

McKee, P (Ed.) (1982). Philosophical foundations of gerontology. New York: Human Sciences Press.

Merton, R. (1949). Discrimination and the American creed. In R. MacIver (Ed.), *Discrimination and National Welfare*. New York: Institute for Religious and Social Studies, Harper & Row.

Merton, R. (1968). *Social theory and social structure*. New York: Free Press.

Mishara, B., & Kastenbaum, R. (1980). *Alcohol and old age*. New York: Grune & Stratton.

Montague, A. (1977). Don't be adultish! *Psychology Today, 11*, 46.

Morris, R. (1989). Challenges of aging in tomorrow's world. *Gerontologist, 29*, 29.

Moss, A., & Lawton, M. (1982). Time budgets of olderpeople. *Journal of Gerontology, 37*, 115.

Musson, N., & Heusinkveld, H. (1963). *Buildings for the elderly*. New York: Reinhold.

Myers, R. (1987). Social Security. In G. Maddox (Ed.), *The encyclopedia of aging*. New York: Springer Publishing Co.

Myers, J., Weissman, M., Tischler, G., Hozer, C., & Leaf, P. (1984). Six months prevalence rates of psychiatric disorders in three communities. *Archives of General Psychiatry, 41*, 959.

Myrdal, G. (1944). *An American dilemma*. New York: Harper & Row.

Nahemow, L., McCluskey-Fawcett, K., & McGhee, P. (Eds.) (1986). *Humor and aging*. New York: Academic Press.

Naisbitt, J. (1982). *Megatrends*. New York: Warner Books.

National Center for Health Statistics. (1977). *Final mortality statistics, 1975* (Vol. 25, No. 11). Washington, DC: U.S. Government Printing Office.

National Center for Health Statistics. (1978). *Current estimates from the health interview survey,* Series 10, No. 126. Washington, DC: U.S. Government Printing Office.

National Center for Health Statistics. (1981). *Health characteristics of persons with chronic activity limitation,* Series 10, No. 137. Washington: DC: U.S. Government Printing Office.

National Center for Health Statistics. (1986). *Vital statistics of the United States, 1983: Life tables.* Washington, DC: U.S. Government Printing Office.

National Center for Health Statistics. (1988). *National Health Survey,* Series 10. Washington DC: U.S. Government Printing Office.

National Safety Council. (1981). *Accident facts.* Chicago: National Safety Council.

Nelson, G. (1983). Tax expenditures for the elderly. *Gerontologist, 23,* 471.

Neugarten, B. (1970). The old and young in modern societies. *American Behavioral Scientist, 14,* 13.

Neugarten, B. (1974). Age groups in American society and the rise of the young old. *Annals of the American Academy* (September) 187.

Neugarten, B. (1977). Personality and aging. In J. Birren & K. Schaie (Eds.), *Handbook of the psychology of aging.* New York: Van Nostrand Reinhold.

Neugarten, B. (Ed.) (1982). *Age or need? Public policies for older people.* Beverly Hills: Sage Publications.

New York Times (1980). How different groups voted for President. November 9, 28.

New York Times (1989). 3 Runners have the times of their lives at 90. November 5, 31.

Newsweek (1982). The third rail of politics. May 24, p. 24.

Nuessel, F. (1982). The language of ageism. *Gerontologist, 22,* 273.

Nusberg, C. (1984). *Innovative aging programs abroad.* Westport, CT: Greenwood Press.

Offenbacher, D., & Poster, C. (1985). Aging and the baseline code: An alternative to the "normless elderly." *Gerontologist, 25,* 526.

Olsen, I. (1982). Attitudes of nursing students toward aging and the aged. *Gerontology and Geriatric Education, 2,* 233.

Oriol, W. (1987). Government programs: Federal. In G. Maddox (Ed.), *The encyclopedia of aging.* New York: Springer Publishing Co.

Osgood, N. (1984). *Suicide in the elderly.* Rockville, MD: Aspen Systems Corporation.

Palmore, E. (1962). Ehtnophaulisms and ethnocentrism. *American Journal of Sociology, 67,* 442.

Palmore, E. (Ed.) (1970). *Normal aging.* Durham, NC: Duke University Press.

Palmore, E. (1971). Attitudes toward aging as shown by humor. *The Gerontologist, 11,* 181.

Palmore, E. (1972a). Medical care needs of the aged. *Postgraduate medicine,* May, 194 & June, 138.

Palmore, E. (1972b). Gerontophobia versus ageism. *Gerontologist, 12,* 213.

Palmore, E. (1972c). Compulsory vs. flexible retirement. *The Gerontologist, 12,* 343.

Palmore, E. (Ed.) (1974). *Normal aging II.* Durham, NC: Duke University Press.

Palmore, E. (1976). The future status of the aged. *Gerontologist, 16,* 297.

Palmore, E. (1977). The facts on aging: A sort quiz. *Gerontologist, 17,* 297.

Palmore, E. (1978a). Are the aged a minority group? *Journal of the American Geriatrics Society, 26,* 214.

Palmore, E. (1978b). When can age, period and cohort be separated? *Social Forces, 57,* 282.

Palmore, E. (1979). Advantages of aging. *Gerontologist, 19,* 220.

Palmore, E. (1981). *Social patterns in normal aging.* Durham, NC: Duke University Press.

Palmore, E. (1982). Attitudes toward the aged. *Research on Aging, 4,* 333.

Palmore, E. (1985). *The honorable elders revisited.* Durham, NC: Duke University Press.

Palmore, E. (1986a). Trends in the health of the aged. *The Gerontologist, 26,* 298.

Palmore, E. (1986b). Attitudes toward aging shown by humor. In L. Nahemo (Ed.), *Humor and aging.* San Diego, CA: Academic Press.

Palmore, E. (1988). *The facts on aging quiz.* New York: Springer Publishing Co.

Palmore, E., Burchett, B., Fillenbaum, G., George, L., & Wallman, L. (1985). *Retirement.* New York: Springer Publishing Co.

Palmore, E., & Maeda, D. (1985). *The honorable elders.* Durham, NC: Duke University Press.

Palmore, E., & Manton, K. (1973). Ageism compared to racism and sexism. *Journal of Gerontology, 28,* 363.

Payne, B. (1984). Protestants. In E. Palmore (Ed.), *Handbook on the aged in the U. S.* Westport, CT: Greenwood Press.

Payne, R., Gibson, F., & Pittard, B. (1969). Social influences in senile psychosis. *Sociological Symposium, 1,* 137.

Pedrick-Cornell, C., & Gelles, R. (1982). Elderly abuse. *Family Relations, 31,* 457.

Pepper, C. (1979). Introduction. In U. S. House Select Committee on Aging, *Federal responsibility to the elderly.* Washington, DC: U.S. Government Printing Office.

Petersen, M. (1973). The visibility and image of old people on television. *Journalism Quarterly, 50,* 569.

Peterson, J. (1987). Foster Grandparent Program. In G. Maddox (Ed.) *The encyclopedia on aging.* New York: Springer Publishing Co.

Peterson, D., & Eden, D. (1977). Teenagers and aging: adolescent literature as an attitude source. *Educational Gerontology, 2,* 311.

Peterson, D., & Karnes, E. (1976). Older people in adolescent literature. *Gerontologist, 16,* 225.

Pfeiffer, E. (1975). A short portable mental status questionaire for the assessment of organic brain deficit in elderly patients. *Journal of the American Geriatrics Society, 23,* 433.

Pfeiffer, E., & Davis, G. (1971). The use of leisure time in middle life. *Gerontologist, 11,* 187.

Polisar, D. (1982). Figurative aging. Paper presented at Southern Sociological Meeting in Memphis, TN, April 1982 (unpublished).

Poon, L. (1987). Learning. In G. Maddox (Ed.), *The encyclopedia of aging.* New York: Springer Publishing Co.

Preston, S. (1984). Children and the elderly in the U.S. *Scientific American, 250,* 44.

Quinn, J. (1987a). Attitude of professionals toward the aged. In G. Maddox (Ed.), *The encyclopedia of aging.* New York: Springer Publishing Co.

Quinn, J. (1987b). Elder abuse and neglect. In G. Maddox (Ed.), *The encyclopedia of aging.* New York: Springer Publishing Co.

Reisberg, B. (1983). *Alzheimer's disease.* New York: Free Press.

Rhodes, S. (1983). Age related differences in work attitudes and behavior. *Psychological Bulletin, 93,* 328.

Richman, J., & Tallmer, M. (1977). The foolishness and wisdom of age: Attitudes toward the elderly as reflected in jokes. *Gerontologist, 17,* 210.

Riesman, D. (1950). *The lonely crowd.* New Haven, CT: Yale University Press.

Riley, M. (1987). Age stratification. In G. Maddox (Ed.), *The encyclopedia of aging.* New York: Springer Publishing Co.

Riley, M., & Foner, A. (1968). *Aging and society, Vol. 1.* New York: Russell Sage.

Ritter, D. (1976). *Ginger Snaps.* Norwalk, CT: C. R. Gibson.

Robin, E. (1977). Old age in elementary school readers. *Educational Gerontology, 2,* 275.

Rockstein, M., & Sussman, M. (1979). *Biology of aging.* Belmont, CA: Wadsworth.

Rokeach, M. (1948). Generalized mental rigidity as a factor in ethnocentrism. *Journal of Abnormal and Social Psychology* (July), 259.

Rokeach, M. (1973). *The nature of human values.* New York: Free Press.

Rokeach, M. (1978). *Understanding human values.* New York: Free Press.

Rose, A. (1969). The subculture of aging. In A. Rose & W. Peterson (Eds.), *Older people and their social world.* Philadelphia: F. A. Davis.

Rosen, B., & Jerdee, T. (1976a). The nature of job-related stereotypes. *Journal of Applied Psychology, 61,* 180.

Rosen, B., & Jerdee, T. (1976b). The influence of age stereotypes on managerial decisions. *Journal of Applied Psychology, 61,* 428.

Rosencranz, H., & McNevin, T. (1969). A factor analysis of attitudes toward the aged. *Gerontologist, 9*, 55.

Rosow, I. (1962). Old age: one moral dilemma of an affluent society. *Gerontologist, 21*, 82.

Rosow, I. (1967). *Social integration of the aged.* New York: Free Press.

Rosow, I. (1974). *Socialization to old age.* Berkeley: University of California Press.

Rosenmayr, L. (1987). On freedom and aging. *Journal of Aging Studies, 1*, 299.

Rosenwaike, I. (1985). *The extreme aged in America.* Westport, CT: Greenwood Press.

Rubin, I. (1968). The "sexless older years"—A socially harmful stereotype. *Annals of the American Academy of Political and Social Sciences, 365*, 86.

Rubenstein, D. (1982). The older person in prison. *Archives of Gerontology and Geriatrics, 1*, 172.

Schick, F. (Ed.) (1986). *Statistical handbook on aging Americans.* Phoenix, AZ: Oryz Press.

Schlesinger, J., & Schlesinger, M. (1981). Aging and opportunities for political office. In S. Kiesler (Ed.), *Aging: Social change.* New York: Academic Press.

Schonfield, D. (1982). Who is stereotyping whom and why? *Gerontologist, 22*, 267.

Schorr, A. (1961). *Filial responsibility in the modern American family.* Washington, DC: U.S. Government Printing Office.

Schulz, J. (1980). *The economics of aging.* Belmont, CA: Wadsworth.

Seefeldt, C., Jantz, R., Galper, A., & Serock, K. (1977). Using pictures to explore children's attitudes toward the elderly. *Gerontologist, 17*, 506.

Seltzer, M., & Atchley, R. (1971). The concept of old: Changing attitudes and stereotypes. *Gerontologist, 11*, 226.

Senate Special Committee on Aging (1988). *Aging America: Trends and projections, 1987–88 Edition.* Washington DC: American Association of Retired Persons.

Siegler, I. (1988). Functional age. In G.Maddox (Ed.), *The encyclopedia of aging.* New York: Springer Publishing Co.

Simpson, G., & Yinger, J. (1985). *Racial and cultural minorities.* New York: Plenum.

Smeeding, T. (1982). *Alternative methods of valuing selected in-kind transfer benefits and measuring their impact on poverty.* Technical Paper No. 50. Washington, DC: Bureau of Census.

Smith, M. (1979). The portrayal of elders in magazine cartoons. *Gerontologist, 19*, 408.

Sohngen, M. (1977). The experience of old age as depicted in contemporary novels. *Gerontologist, 17*, 70.

Soldo, B., & Manton, K. (1983). Health service needs of the oldest old. *Millbank Memorial Fund Quarterly: Health and Society, 63* (2), 266.

Sontag, S. (1972). The double standard of aging. *Saturday Review of the Society* (September 23), 30.

Stannard, C. (1973). Old folks and dirty work: The social conditions for patient abuse in a nursing home. *Social Problems, 20,* 329.

Starr, B., & Weiner, M. (1981). *Sex and sexuality in the mature years.* New York: McGraw-Hill.

Stein, E. (Date unknown). What is ageism? Unpublished sheet (mimeographed) Place unknown.

Stephens, J. (1976). *Loners, losers, and lovers: Elderly tenants in a slum hotel.* Seattle, WA: University of Washington Press.

Stephens, R. (1989). FAA: It's flying blind. *AARP Bulletin, 30* (# 9, October), 1.

Stewart, M., & Ryan, E. (1982). Attitudes toward younger and older adult speakers. *Journal of Language and Social Psychology, 1,* 91.

Storck, P., & Cutler, M. (1977). Pictorial representation of adults as observed in children's literature. *Educational Gerontology, 2,* 293.

Streib, G. (1965). Are the aged a minority group? In A. Gouldner, & S. Miller, (Eds.), *Applied Sociology.* New York: Free Press.

Sullivan, P., & Adelson, J. (1954). Ethnocentrism and misanthropy. *Journal of Abnormal and Social Psychology* (April), 246.

Taves, M., & Hansen, G. (1963). Seventeen hundred elderly citizens. In A. Rose (Ed.), *Aging in Minnesota.* Minneapolis: University of Minnesota Press.

Terry, R., & Katzman, R. (1983). Senile dementia of the Alzheimer's type. *Annals of Neurology, 14,* 497.

Thobaden, M., & Anderson, L. (1985). Reporting elder abuse. *American Journal of Nursing, 85,* 371.

Thomas, E., & Yamamoto, K. (1975). Attitudes toward age: an exploration in school-age children. *The International Journal of Aging and Human Development, 6,* 117.

Thorson, J., Whatley, L., and Hancock, K. (1974). Attitudes toward the aged as a function of age and education. *Gerontologist, 14,* 316.

Tibbitts, C. (1979). Can we invalidate negative stereotypes in aging? *Gerontologist, 22,* 10.

Torrey, B. (1982). Guns vs. canes: The fiscal implication of an aging population. *American Economic Review, 72,* 309.

Townsend, P. (1968). Isolation, desolation, and loneliness. In E. Shana, et al. (Eds.), *Old people in three industrial societies.* New York: Atherton.

Tuckman, J., & Lorge, I. (1953). Attitudes toward old people. *Journal of Social Psychology, 37,* 249.

Tuckman, J., & Lorge, I. (1958). The projection of personal symptoms into stereotypes about aging. *Journal of Gerontology, 13,* 70.

Turner, B., & Kahn, R. (1974). Age as a political issue. *Journal of Gerontology, 29,* 572.

U.S. Bureau of the Census. (1981). *U.S. Current Population Reports, Series P-20, No. 147.* Washington, DC: U.S. Government Printing Office.

U.S. Bureau of the Census. (1984a). Demographic and socioeconomic aspects of aging in the U.S. *U.S. Current Population Reports, Series P-23, No. 138.* Washington, DC: U.S. Government Printing Office.

U.S. Bureau of the Census. (1984b). Projections of the population of the United States, by age, sex, and race: 1983 to 2080. *U.S. Current Population Reports, Series P-23, No. 952.* Washington, DC: U.S. Government Printing Office.

U.S. Commision on Civil Rights. (1977 & 1979). *The age discrimination study, Parts I & II.* Washington, DC: The Commission.

U.S. Department of Health, Education, and Welfare. (1983). Medical program, hospice care. *Federal Register, 48,* 56008.

U.S. Department of Justice. (1983). *Crime in the United States.* Washington, DC: U.S. Government Printing Office.

U.S. House Select Committee on Aging. (1981). *Elder abuse: An examination of a hidden problem.* Washington, DC: U.S. Government Printing Office.

U.S. Senate Special Committee on Aging. (1965). *Frauds and deceptions affecting the elderly.* Washington, DC: U.S. Government Printing Office.

U.S. Senate Special Committee on Aging. (1985). *Developments in aging: 1984.* (Vol. 1). Washington, DC: U.S. Government Printing Office.

U.S. Senate Special Committee on Aging. (1986). *Developments in aging: 1986.* (Vol. 1). Washington, DC: U.S. Government Printing Office.

U.S. Senate Special Committee on Aging. (1988). *Aging America: Trends and projections.* Washington: DC: U.S. Government Printing Office.

Verba, S., & Nie, N. (1972). *Participation in America.* New York: Harper & Row.

Vickio, C., & Cavanaugh, J. (1985). Relationships among death anxiety, attitudes toward aging, and experience with death among nursing home employees. *Journal of Gerontology, 40,* 347.

Vinick, B. (1979). Remarriage. In R. Jacobs and B. Vinick (Eds.), *Reengagement in later life.* Stamford, CT: Greylock.

Waxman, H., & Carner, E. (1984). Physician recognition, diagnosis, and treatment of mental disorders in elderly medical patients. *Gerontologist, 24,* 593.

Webster's ninth new collegiate dictionary. (1987). Springfield, MA: Merriam-Webster, Inc.

Wernick, M., & Manaster, G. (1984). Age and perception of age and attractiveness. *Gerontologist, 24,* 409.

Whittington, F. (1987). Drug abuse. In G. Maddox (Ed.), *The encyclopedia of aging.* New York: Springer Publishing Co.

Williams, R. (1960). *American society* (2nd edition). New York: Knopf.

Williams, R., Dean, J., & Suchman, E. (1964). *Strangers next door.* New York: Prentice-Hall.

Williamson, J., Evans, L., & Nunley, A. (1980). *Aging and society.* New York: Holt, Rinehart, & Winston.

Wood, W. (1987). Alcoholism. In G. Maddox (Ed.), *The encyclopedia of aging.* New York: Springer Publishing Co.

Index